D0966705

Advance Praise for *Agile Selling*

"In a business environment where sales intelligence matters, *Agile Selling* provides a blueprint for quickly becoming an invaluable resource to prospects and customers. Use these strategies to increase your sales team's productivity and drive rapid revenue growth."

—Umberto Milletti, CEO, InsideView

"Any small-business owner ready to hire a salesperson needs to read *Agile Selling* by Jill Konrath. This book will give you a road map for how to get your salesperson up and running quickly, adding revenue to the bottom line."

—Melinda F. Emerson, "SmallBizLady," author of
Become Your Own Boss in 12 Months

"Your sales force is key to fast growth in today's evolving economy. *Agile Selling* will give you the tools and strategies to increase sales productivity, minimize turnover, and drive more revenue, giving you a competitive edge."

—Verne Harnish, CEO, Gazelles; author of
The Greatest Business Decisions of All Time

"Jill has captured one of the key pivots salespeople need to make in the new sales world. This book is for top producers or those who want to be, those people who want to be trusted advisers, not just transaction processors and service reps. Follow these insights to turn yourself into the 'go to' source for solving your customers' business problems and the provider of choice for their bigger buys."

—Tom Searcy, CEO, Hunt Big Sales; bestselling coauthor of
How to Close a Deal Like Warren Buffett

"Today, successful sales isn't really about 'selling' in the classic sense. It's about helping, making yourself a valuable resource to the industry and to prospective customers. In *Agile Selling*, Jill Konrath has created the definitive modern playbook for creating new business opportunities. I promise you'll read it at least twice."

—Jay Baer, *New York Times* bestselling author of
Youtility: Why Smart Marketing Is About Help, Not Hype

"Every seller needs to read *Agile Selling* right now to learn how to adapt their selling and learning skills to handle the increasingly rapid pace of change. Jill serves up priceless gems of wisdom that are both practical and immediately impactful. This book is excellent."
—Donal Daly, CEO, The TAS Group; author of
Account Planning in Salesforce

"Refreshingly honest and relentlessly practical."
—Olivia Fox Cabane, author of *The Charisma Myth*

"*Agile Selling* is about great sales professionals. Jill looks at what makes them different, how they work, what they do, how they do it, what sets them apart, and what makes them great. This is not a 'how to do' book, it is a 'how to be' book—possibly the single most important one anyone aspiring to be a great sales professional can read."
—Dave Brock, CEO, Partners in Excellence

"*Agile Selling* is an onboarding bible! The time it takes to ramp up new sales reps can be measured in lost revenue. This book provides both individuals and organizations with a way to assimilate information and learn the new skills they'll need to become valuable to their buyers more quickly. It rocks!"   —Trish Bertuzzi, CEO, The Bridge Group

"*Agile Selling* is a crucial guide for the new age of salespeople. Konrath has written a book full of practical and extremely usable practices that everyone in sales, both those just starting out and those with years of experience, should read immediately."
—Mike Schultz, president, RAIN Group; coauthor of *Insight Selling*

"When Jill first told me about *Agile Selling*, I immediately thought there is no better person to write about that subject. She's the most agile person I know. Later, when I read the manuscript, I was simply floored. This book is a treasure trove of knowledge about a critical capability for sales professionals and, surprisingly, one that has not been written about before. As always, Jill has done a masterful job. This is a *must-read*."
—Dave Stein, CEO and founder, ES Research Group

"I became a huge fan of Jill's when over a thousand of her raving fans signed up to hear her speak at our record-breaking Inside Sales Virtual Summit, the most of any of our sixty-two sales experts. In her third exciting book, Jill captures why some succeed in sales and others don't—agility. *Agile Selling* convincingly makes the case for the *agile* mind-set and shares eighteen quick-learning strategies, eighteen causal new skills, and eighteen gritty success habits you must know to turn obstacles into opportunities."

—Ken Krogue, founder and president, InsideSales.com;
weekly contributor on Forbes.com;
no. 1 world-ranked blogger on inside sales

"Whether you are new to your sales role or an experienced salesperson, *Agile Selling* is *the* book to make you maximally effective in the shortest time possible. From learning new information quickly to tackling your personal sales challenges, this book offers proven tactics and tools to focus on what matters most to you and your customers."

—Kendra Lee, president, KLA Group; author of
The Sales Magnet and *Selling Against the Goal*

"*Agile Selling* provides the new master entrepreneur skill. The pace of change in all facets of business means those who can adapt the fastest win!"

—John Jantsch, author of
Duct Tape Marketing and *Duct Tape Selling*

"Dozens of books give you yet another new system or methodology to jump-start your sales. But if you want to get better now—and keep getting better in the future—you need to know how to create value for your clients in the blitzkrieg of never-ending and disruptive change. In sixty-three zippy chapters, *Agile Selling* will give you superpowers you didn't know you needed so that you can be the differentiator that your clients and customers want." —Anthony Iannarino, author of *The Sales Blog*

"*Agile Selling* is a must-read book for all new reps coming into a sales team. Today's seller must know how to learn and how to change on the fly. It's written in an easy manner with dozens of examples throughout. Definitely the most important book Jill Konrath has authored so far."

—Lori Richardson, CEO, Score More Sales

"Jill Konrath's bestselling *Selling to Big Companies* and *SNAP Selling* solidified her position as a thought leader in the sales space. It's my view that *Agile Selling* will surpass the success of both these books, simply because it doesn't just address issues facing frontline sellers today, but also those in the future. She shows us how to avoid commoditization, expand our commercial bandwidth, and actually thrive—even in challenging times."

—Jonathan Farrington, CEO, Top Sales World;
managing partner, Jonathan Farrington & Associates

"I didn't think Jill could outdo *SNAP Selling*—but she does in this new book, diving into how the brain works and its ability to rapidly learn new information and skills. Whether you're new to your job or a journeyman sales professional, you'll walk away with great insight into how to accomplish more in less time. Combining solid advice on selling strategies, techniques, and management, Jill again has produced a major hit!"

—Michael J. Nick, CEO, ROI4Sales, Inc.; author of *The Key to the C-Suite*

"In a world where buyers are empowered with online and social media information, what role is left for salespeople? Jill's analysis points to the agile seller: individuals who learn rapidly, know their buyer intimately, and transcend what they sell to become creators of business value. Willy Loman and *Glengarry Glen Ross* be damned: the new buying and selling environment has no place for you. This new breed—the agile seller—is the hero of the new economy."

—Steve Richard, managing partner, Vorsight

"If you're a small business who wants to grow, *Agile Selling* is a compelling read. Jill has a powerful ability to share the mind-set, tools, and techniques needed for success with today's savvy buyers. If you're hiring salespeople—or want to get better yourself—read this book."

—Anita Campbell, CEO, Small Business Trends

"Have you noticed that buyers have changed? They self-educate and, when ready to buy, call you to negotiate and grind on price. If anyone knows what to do about this, it's Jill. Want to increase sales? Get inside this book. Fresh, fast, and focused . . . it is exceptionally well written."

—Oren Klaff, bestselling author of *Pitch Anything*

"The marketplace is changing rapidly and it can be a challenge to stay ahead. Jill Konrath provides tactical, on-the-ground advice for quickly understanding and effectively fulfilling the needs of your customers."

—Todd Henry, author of *Die Empty*

AGILE SELLING

ALSO BY JILL KONRATH

SNAP Selling
Selling to Big Companies

AGILE
SELLING

Getting Up to Speed Quickly in Today's
Ever-Changing Sales World

JILL KONRATH

PORTFOLIO / PENGUIN

PORTFOLIO / PENGUIN
Published by the Penguin Group
Penguin Group (USA) LLC
375 Hudson Street
New York, New York 10014

USA | Canada | UK | Ireland | Australia | New Zealand | India | South Africa | China
penguin.com
A Penguin Random House Company

First published by Portfolio / Penguin, a member of Penguin Group (USA) LLC, 2014

Library of Congress Cataloging-in-Publication Data
Konrath, Jill.
Agile selling : get up to speed quickly in today's ever-changing sales world / Jill Konrath.
pages cm
Includes index.
ISBN 978-1-59184-725-0
1. Selling. I. Title.
HF5438.25.K6598 2014
658.85—dc23
2014004248

Printed in the United States of America
1 3 5 7 9 10 8 6 4 2

Set in Miller Text
Designed by Alissa Rose Theodor

May you live an abundant life

CONTENTS

PART 5: Success Habits of Agile Sellers

PART 6: Final Words

AGILE SELLING

INTRODUCTION

Why did it take me so many years to find out what really matters for sales success? Despite having been in the field for decades, I'm not being facetious when I ask that. It's only within the past few years that I've gained the wisdom and perspective to see what really differentiates those who excel in sales from everyone else.

First, a little background. I've been on the "sales effectiveness" bandwagon for umpteen years. In my role as a sales consultant, I've helped salespeople with strategies and tactics they can use to create new opportunities, speed up sales cycles, jump-start new product sales, and expand business in existing accounts. I've even written two bestselling books on the topic: *SNAP Selling,* a step-by-step guide to winning deals with today's frazzled customers, and *Selling to Big Companies,* which details how to set up meetings with corporate decision makers. The practices outlined in those books have been immensely helpful to tens of thousands of sellers who needed this guidance.

Yet I've painted an incomplete picture. Not on purpose, but because of my own blindness to so many things I've unwittingly done that have contributed to my success.

All that changed on the day in 2011 when Andrew Limouris, CEO of Medix, asked me to talk to his young sales force about my early years in sales. He wanted me to share my perceptions on why I'd succeeded when so many others had failed.

"Mmm," I thought. "Why did I?" As I pondered the question, I was struck with a realization. There were so many other factors, beyond sales skills, that contributed to my success—like how I dealt with fear, my never-fail mind-set, and thinking from my customer's perspective. Because these were just "things" I did, I had totally disregarded their importance. Yet on reflection, they were key contributors to my success.

Since that fateful day three years ago, I've continued to research and deepen my knowledge of what makes salespeople successful. I've queried top performers to learn more about their strategies. I've studied developments in neuroscience to understand how our brain works—and even learned about how our normal "way of working" actually impedes our success. And I've delved into my own career to mine the golden nuggets.

Above all, I realized that my abilities *to get up to speed quickly and rapidly adapt to changing conditions* were what mattered most. Success was contingent on my sales agility—the mind-set and skills I developed that allowed me to rapidly acquire knowledge and develop new skills, combined with the flexibility and strength needed to withstand challenges and leap on opportunities.

You've probably never heard anyone talk about sales agility before. Sales training programs don't even mention the word. But every top seller I know is an agile learner who knows what it takes to dive into a new situation and figure it out quickly.

There's no reason you should be stumbling around trying to

crack the elusive sales code when you don't have to. You can actually learn these agile strategies; there's no magic involved. When you apply these strategies to your sales career, they make all the difference in the world.

So who should read this book? I wrote it for everyone with untapped sales potential who could be so much better than they are today. I'm talking about:

- Experienced sellers who want to jump-start success in their new sales position.
- New salespeople who haven't yet figured out what it takes to succeed.
- Struggling salespeople who want to take their game to a new level.
- Committed entrepreneurs who have a tough time getting new clients.

If you fall into any of the categories above, I guarantee you'll find this book useful for both your short-term and long-term success. Now, I know you're busy selling at this very moment, which is why I kept this book short and snappy, but if you follow the teachings here, you'll find out how to be so much more productive, effective, and best of all, agile.

Let me give you a snapshot of what's coming.

In Part 1: The Case for Agile, you'll discover just how much today's buyers have changed. You'll discover the key to differentiating and winning business in a highly competitive marketplace and find out why your learning agility is the ultimate key to your sales success.

In Part 2: The Agile Mind-set, you will learn about the mentality that helps you get better faster, at the same time as it prevents you from failing. I will also unveil strategies to get you in the right frame of mind for sales success. If you've just taken a new sales position or even just started selling, these insights will keep you afloat while you're learning.

In Part 3: Learn New Info Quickly, you'll determine how top sellers quickly acquire the depth of knowledge they need to earn situational credibility in just thirty days. This section helps you define what you need to learn, the proper sequence for absorbing new information, and how to make the new knowledge stick in your brain. (If you've just started at a new company or need to launch a new product, go immediately to this section. It will be a lifesaver for you.)

In Part 4: Pick Up New Skills Fast, you'll read about all sorts of strategies you can use to get better at selling in record time. This section isn't just for newbies; with today's changing buyer expectations, virtually every seller needs to upgrade his or her skills to approach prospects and close deals. And if your company has a new product or service, you'll want a quick refresher to ensure that what you're doing is maximally effective.

In Part 5: Success Habits of Agile Sellers, you'll discover numerous ways to tackle the challenges you inevitably face. The section is a veritable gold mine of tips you can use to motivate yourself, strengthen your skills, manage your time, and overcome your shortfalls. Again, savvy sellers are constantly searching for ways to optimize their time and free up resources for high-value activities.

You don't need to read every line in this book to see results. Personally, I think chapter 6 can alter your life. Then again, so could chapter 15 or chapter 50. There's a wealth of tools and techniques here that can fundamentally shift your sales thinking, and ultimately your results. The more you embrace these ideas and strategies, the higher your likelihood of both immediate success and long-term mastery.

Time to get learning!

Part 1

The Case for Agile

In a world of continuous change and perceived product/service parity, sellers are the key differentiator. Their learning agility becomes a key factor in their success.

1

CHANGE, CHANGE, AND MORE CHANGE

A gile. Responsive to change. Fleet-footed. Quick-witted. Able to turn on a dime.

I can't think of better words to describe the characteristics needed by people in sales today.

We're working in a world of unrelenting change, much of it totally beyond our control. Yet as sellers, we have to adjust to it, sometimes literally overnight. To further complicate things, we have to do it at the same time we're trying to achieve our sales goals. It's a daunting task, especially when you think of the massive changes we're facing.

For starters, take a look at your own company. It's probably in constant flux, even if you're a small business. Every year, new products and services are brought to market and new strategic initiatives are introduced. Priorities shift frequently, compensation plans are altered, and new bosses come in with different expectations. It's likely that you've dealt with some major reorganization of your company or team in the past year too.

Add to this all the new technology you're expected to use on the job: CRM (customer relationship management) systems, online meetings, social networks, alert services, lead generation software, collaboration tools, and smart phone apps, to name a few. This alone brings many sellers to their knees, begging for relief. When you combine this with all the data you're being bombarded with on a daily basis, it's a sure setup for feeling massively overwhelmed.

That's only part of the picture. The marketplace changes as well. Entire industries collapse, while new ones emerge. Our volatile economy either tumbles or booms. Interest rates go up and down. Legislation alters market dynamics. Political and economic unrest on the other side of the world affects decisions being made locally. You can't influence any of these things, yet they have a huge impact on your success. And, we haven't even addressed the biggest elephant in the room yet—changing buyer behavior.

Phew! It's impossible to stay on top of it all. So much to learn in so little time. And it just keeps coming at you. As soon as you think you've got it all figured out, BAM, more change and you're scrambling again.

Adapting to this much change can be painful. Rather than feeling agile, you feel inept and clumsy. Achieving proficiency seems unattainable and unsustainable. When you take a new job, the situation is compounded exponentially. Not only do you have to get up to speed on just about everything, but you may also have to learn how to sell for the first time.

Constant change is the new normal. As sellers, we're challenged to figure out how to thrive in this ever-evolving ecosystem.

You don't have to be at the mercy of all this change. By focusing on new mind-sets, rapid learning strategies, and fresh ways to acquire new sales skills, you can thrive in this environment.

> It's tough to be proficient in a changing environment.

2

UNDERSTANDING TODAY'S BUYER

If you're frustrated dealing with today's prospects, join the crowd. It's hard to do your job when no one returns your calls or responds to your e-mails. It's exasperating when you invest tons of time with a hot prospect and then he or she decides to stay with the status quo. And when it's finally time to ink the deal, it seems like all your prospects care about is price.

Buyers have changed: fundamentally, drastically, and for good. They don't need you anymore. When they have an issue, they go online to research their problem. They check multitudes of Web sites, looking for information that can help them understand their challenge, how others are solving it, opinions on best solutions, and more. They download white papers, attend online events, read articles, listen to audios, and check out forums.

In short, buyers self-educate, leaving the seller totally out of the loop. When they finally decide to engage, they're often 60 to 70 percent of the way through their buying process! It's only when they know what they want that they call in a few vendors and start negotiating.

Why do buyers keep sellers out? Because in their experience, most are product-pushing peddlers who don't bring any value to the decision process, ask stupid questions, offer minimal insights, and give boring presentations. The last thing they want to do is waste their precious time caught in a meeting with another self-serving salesperson. They're simply too busy for that.

You may think you're different. Buyers don't.

To get on someone's calendar, keep their attention, win deals, and ensure loyalty, you need to understand and deliver what today's buyers want. Your success depends on:

- Knowing more. Buyers expect you to understand their business, direction, challenges, processes, and relationship history.

- Providing value. Every single interaction is evaluated to determine if it is worth the time or effort. Buyers want ideas, insights, leadership, and guidance to assess whether changing makes sense and how to do it best.

- Meeting them where they're at. You're expected to provide what buyers need, when they want it, and how they want it, quickly.

As sellers, we may think we're doing all these things. Unfortunately, our buyers beg to differ. According to a recent survey by Forrester Research, only 15 percent of executives say their meetings with salespeople met their expectations. From that, only 7 percent of execs actually scheduled follow-up conversations. Ouch. That's not good!

Clearly, the bar for salespeople has been raised. Today's buyers have more power than ever before. Unless we meet their expectations, they won't talk with us or buy from us. In many cases, this is a gap of epic proportions. Sellers have learned about their products or services, but remain uneducated about many things that are important to buyers. But what are those things? And how can sellers learn them quickly?

Without deep buyer understanding, it's increasingly difficult to get business. This is the information that fuels sellers' ability to provide value in their interactions, a key requisite for winning more business. The nature of the interaction needs to change too. You're dealing with educated people who want conversations and collaboration, not pitches of any sort.

Here's the good news. What today's buyers are requesting is not impossible. Every single seller is capable of doing what's necessary. When you do, you get radically different responses.

According to the Aberdeen Group, companies whose salespeople leveraged online resources to learn about prospects saw revenue jump over 21 percent. In CEB's studies, sellers who challenged customers' thinking and brought them fresh insights significantly outperformed their colleagues.

These findings show that engaged, knowledgeable sellers clearly have an important place in today's marketplace. Providing value may look different today, but once you know what buyers expect, it's certainly doable.

As sellers, we need to up our game and become the person our customers want to deal with. Stop doing what's no longer effective and embrace this challenge.

> Buyers' expectations have changed;
> sellers need to provide value.

3

BE THE DIFFERENTIATOR

The sales opportunities today are far bigger than you might realize. Research shows that in a world of nearly identical products and services, sellers and buyers have very different perceptions about what influences purchase decisions and customer loyalty.

Salespeople invariably cite pricing, brand, and the product or service itself as the most important factors. They often feel that things totally outside their control thwart their own best efforts. This belief is the source of lots of finger-pointing and blame.

You know what buyers pick as the differentiator in their decisions? The sales experience* itself—what it's like working with you during the course of all your interactions. They think this experience as a whole is more important than all the other factors combined.

---

* Source: Sales Executive Council Research, 2011. Impact of B2B Customer Loyalty Drivers: 19 percent company and brand impact, 19 percent product and service delivery, 9 percent value-to-price ratio, and 53 percent sales experience.

Buyers are saying that sellers are the primary differentiator. That means *you* matter—more than what you sell, what it costs, and whom you work for. They choose you, or, if you don't do a good enough job, they choose your competitor. Only if no salesperson stands out from the crowd do they use pricing, products, or brand as differentiating elements in their decision making.

This should get you excited. Finally, something you have total control over—the sales experience you deliver! Every day you can get up knowing that what you know and how you leverage it is the biggest factor in your success.

Still, there's so much you don't know. Sure, you have a fairly good understanding of your product and service, but that's not high on your prospects' list of things they care about. They want you to know their business. They want you to help them figure things out. They want ideas, insights, and information that you don't necessarily have right now. If you're new in the job, it's like you got hit with a double whammy.

Here's what it all boils down to: To become the differentiator, you need to always be learning. Sometimes just the sheer magnitude of what I need to learn makes me want to hyperventilate. There are days when I wish that someone would pry open my brain and pour everything I need to know inside. Just because I've been in sales for years doesn't make me immune to all these changes. Sometimes it makes it even worse because I have more to unlearn.

I suspect you feel the same way. We need to be smarter now

than we've ever been before. We need to provide value in every conversation and manage the customer experience.

How we sell is more important than what we sell. It's totally within our power to become the person whom our prospects choose to buy from.

> Turn yourself into the primary differentiator.

4

THE AGILE IMPERATIVE

Sales has now officially become a thinking-intensive profession. We need to learn a lot fast, and figure out how to best integrate our knowledge into our customer interactions. We need to be quick, nimble, and responsive to the never-ending volatility we encounter from every direction.

Unfortunately, our brain doesn't always cooperate. It likes routines, getting things down pat. As soon as it sees us repeating the same behaviors, it systematizes these actions. Pretty soon, our prospecting messages, conversations, and presentations all start sounding alike. We're operating on autopilot and don't even know it.

The more we use these routines, the harder they are to change. Our self-created rut becomes increasingly difficult to escape from. As we start slipping behind, it gets harder and harder to meet our sales goals. It also gets harder to learn new things.

The truth is, in today's business environment, learning agility matters. We can never know enough. When change happens, we need to be able to turn on a dime. For example, one of my clients just announced that they were going upmarket, targeting significantly larger companies than their sales reps had ever called on before. Another client just came out with a new product that pits them against a formidable competitor they've never gone head-to-head with. A third client is being impacted by recent legislative changes. In all cases, their salespeople need to figure out new approaches to deal with the new market dynamics—quickly, if they're going to meet their numbers.

Sometimes you create your own change too, especially in taking on a new job. One day you're selling technology services to VPs of marketing and the next day you're selling capital equipment to plant managers. Even though you may already have tons of sales experience, you still have so much to learn. And every single seller I know wants to ramp up and achieve proficiency as soon as humanly possible.

According to research by Korn/Ferry International, "Learning agility is a leading predictor of leadership success today—more reliable than IQ, EQ [emotional intelligence] or even leadership competencies."

The same is true in sales. Learning agility becomes your competitive advantage. It's what enables you to be the differentiator. Of course, being agile requires that you spend time thinking about what changes are occurring, what they mean, what you need to know now, and finally, the best way to take action.

If you're an agile learner, you're resourceful, adaptable, and proactive. You're ready to tackle your customers' biggest challenges and help them succeed. It means you're a skilled communicator because you've learned to think from other people's perspectives. You're fast and flexible in the ideas you generate, and are able to come up with lots of ways to achieve your goals.

Your sales success depends on quickly assimilating information and mastering new skills, and learning agility is the key meta-skill that makes this success possible. It enables you to rise above the complexity to find fresh solutions, extrapolate from one situation to the next, and deal with moving targets. If you're an agile learner, you're ready to keep testing and searching for the right answers, knowing that they're out there to be found. You can sense threats and opportunities early on, when you can still alter the outcome.

When you're an agile learner, you close more sales faster, with higher margins. It's worth acquiring this meta-skill for that one reason alone. But it's also a life skill that will help you no matter where you work and for whom. People who can get up to speed quickly, in any industry and any job, are in high demand.

Clearly, that's a compelling imperative to develop your learning agility. There's also a need to understand the mind-set that provides the underpinnings needed to acquire and sustain this mental nimbleness. Top sellers aren't just rapid and avid learners. They have a mind-set that propels them enthusiastically forward despite the challenges that lie in their path. Fortunately, as you'll soon see, you can adopt this invaluable belief system too.

> Learning agility is your only sustainable competitive advantage.

Part 2

The Agile Mind-set

Agile sellers think differently from their peers. This mind-set keeps them going through challenging times and ultimately leads to mastery.

5

MAKE THE PIVOTAL DECISION

As you well know, getting good at anything takes time and effort. You're virtually guaranteed to run into bumps along the way. Some obstacles will seem insurmountable. There will be days and weeks when you'll have serious doubts about your company and your capabilities.

I've encountered these feelings many times in my career. Fear, uncertainty, and doubt always seem to rear their ugly heads whenever you're faced with a steep learning curve. In *The War of Art*, Steven Pressfield calls this the "resistance." He defines it as "an invisible force that opposes you any time you try to accomplish something significant or make any improvement in any area of your life." While it may be invisible, it sure is powerful.

I remember one of my first major battles with the resistance. I was totally new to sales and had just started selling copiers for Xerox. As part of our training, every new salesperson had to memorize a twenty-minute demonstration—verbatim. Years later, it's still ingrained in my brain:

"Mr. Prospect, for years Xerox designed copiers to satisfy

the needs and requirements of our customers. Our experience and success show us that there are four basic criteria that must be met: ease of operation, copy quality, reliability, and flexibility. Is there anything else that's important to you, Mr. Prospect? . . ."

After weeks of practice, I was finally ready for prime time. As soon as Bob, my prospect, was standing in front of the copier at our demo facility, I started right in on my script and kept on going, not missing a single word. I nailed the demonstration.

The final line of the demo, before we asked for the order, was: "Any questions? Comments?" When I said that, Bob looked right at me, smiled, and said: "It looks good, Jill. But my name is not Mr. Prospect."

I was mortified and wanted to quit right then and there. But I didn't. This marked a pivotal moment for my sales career. I had to either make it at Xerox or find another position and start all over again. I chose to stay—and it changed my life.

What many sellers don't realize is that success is a choice. It's not a God-given right nor is it based on your natural talents. I know countless "normal" people who succeeded simply because they said to themselves, "Doggone it. I'm going to figure this thing out."

Conversely, I've seen exceptionally talented individuals get totally discouraged with sales. It was much harder than they'd expected. Rather than making the pivotal decision, they quit on themselves. They chose to sink and not swim. Ultimately, they achieved only a fraction of what they were capable of achieving and left the job, discouraged and feeling like losers.

As we strive for competence, it's normal to be plagued by fear, uncertainty, and doubt. These emotions whisper to us that we'll never figure it out, that the struggle isn't worth it, and that it's not our fault if we fail. It happens to everyone. Unfortunately, too many people let the resistance win.

Recently, I spoke to a group of high-achieving salespeople about the mind-set necessary for sales success. I shared with them how often I'd worried myself sick about meeting my numbers or making it in a new position. (Nobody would have guessed it since I put up a good front.) As I talked about my battle with the resistance, I was stunned to see every single head in the room bobbing up and down, ever so slightly. They all felt it too. You'd never have known it because they all looked so darn confident and competent. But then again, so did I.

Agile sellers refuse to let fear, uncertainty, and doubt win. While they don't like how the resistance makes them feel, they accept that it's a normal part of the learning process. More important, this acceptance propels them forward. They want to be proficient as fast as they can, and to get there, they throw themselves into learning.

They've made the pivotal choice. They're not hoping or trying to be successful; they've chosen it deliberately. This mind-set keeps them going through the tough times, proof positive that it matters.

> Success is a decision.
> Dare to choose it.

6

TRANSFORM SALES PROBLEMS

A gile sellers see problems differently. First off, they're expecting difficulties to arise so they aren't surprised when they do. Because they're prepared for challenges, they don't let obstacles and complications suck the energy out of them.

Not sure what I mean by that? Think of how you feel after hearing that your best prospect is going to be inking a deal with your competitor. Stymied? Deflated? Like you've been punched in the stomach? Add in a little pressure—both self-induced and from your boss—and these feelings get even worse.

Losing your oomph is bad for business. Your brain literally shuts down on you, making it even harder to figure out what to do. There's a biological reason for this; under stress, your body produces way too much cortisol. This hormone degrades your memory, shrinks your ability to generate creative options, and makes you feel like success is totally out of your control.

The key is to shift your perspective and stop seeing problems as something to fear. While this isn't easy, it's transformative.

Years ago, I faced a huge career crisis after losing two big clients. Both, under pressure from Wall Street, had cut all extraneous expenses. My projects as a consultant to them evaporated overnight. My clients said, "Hang in there, Jill. We'll restart soon." They never did.

Suddenly, I was thrust back into prospecting mode again. I quickly discovered that the approach I had used with great success for many years was grossly ineffective. At first, I was frustrated, but as time went on, my fears started running rampant. I worried that I'd lost my mojo and no one would ever hire me again. After all, who wants to work with a sales consultant who can't get clients? Finally, I started asking other salespeople and entrepreneurs if they were having problems. It was like opening a floodgate. It turned out that everyone I spoke to was struggling.

Once I realized that it wasn't just me, a lightbulb went on. Suddenly I realized that viewing my situation as a problem was sapping my creative energy. Even when well-intentioned friends offered good ideas, I was pessimistic and dismissive. I was caught in a downward spiral of negativity. Just when I needed all the brainpower I could muster, it was totally unavailable to me.

Everything changed when I turned my problem into a challenge. I said to myself: *Jill, this is a challenge. You don't know the solution, but you're good at solving puzzles. You can figure this out.*

When I did that, a few things happened immediately. I regained a sense of control over my future and my brain started working again. I became curious and started asking myself lots of questions: Why weren't prospects responding? If I altered my message, would I get different responses? Did I know enough to sound credible? Would I delete myself? Was I quitting too soon?

Ultimately, I found the solution—and then wrote *Selling to Big Companies* so others could benefit from what I'd learned.

My experience isn't unique. Neuroscience research shows that when you make a mental shift to view obstacles as opportunities, your brain is reenergized. It loves challenges and immediately starts scanning the environment, looking for insights that you might find useful. It also starts digging into your past, looking for previous experiences you've had that might be helpful. Suddenly, you find relevant information that you totally overlooked when you were wallowing in the mud. Maybe you'll be reading an article online that's not really even relevant to your specific challenge, but it will trigger a new prospecting idea. Or you'll get up in the morning with a fresh perspective on how to address a difficult situation. Good ideas seem to appear out of nowhere when your brain is in this state.

For most people, creating challenges out of problems is not a natural habit. But, as I've discovered, it's what agile sellers do on a regular basis. They know that this mind-set frees up their creative energy so they can come up with solutions to their problems.

Transform your problems into challenges.

7

REFRAME FAILURE

Another mind-set that agile sellers possess is the ability to see failure differently. When a competitor wins a deal, agile sellers refuse to see themselves as the loser. When they fall into slumps, as we all do, they don't take it as an indication of their competence. In short, failure isn't one bit personal.

Recently, I was listening to an interview with Sara Blakely, CEO of Spanx and the world's youngest female billionaire. She started her company in 2000, overcoming tremendous odds to turn her dream into a reality. When asked what made her successful, she said it was the question her father asked every single night at dinner: "What did you fail at today?" If she hadn't failed at something, her dad was disappointed. It was a sign she wasn't growing, learning, or stretching to her potential.

Agile sellers don't see failure as an indictment of their capabilities. They see it as a natural part of the learning process. They expect to make mistakes and assume they'll screw up. That doesn't mean they like it any more than you or I do. But they know that whenever they start a job, they'll be given many valuable learning experiences.

Personally, I've chosen to follow their example. Over the years, I've failed often. Sometimes these were minor fails, but other times, they were whoppers. I'll never forget the rookie mistake I made that totally offended Tinsey, the CEO's assistant. When I first spoke to her, Tinsey told me that she made the final copier decision for the office—she was my buyer. But the weekend after I spoke with her, I read a sales book that stated it was crucial for me to sell to Mr. Big, not a lowly underling. So first thing Monday morning, I called and got an appointment with the CEO.

When I arrived for my meeting with the CEO, Tinsey met me as I came in the door. She was furious about what I'd done and verbally attacked me with a vengeance. Four-letter words were flying. In shock, I fainted dead away in the lobby. I literally had to pick myself up off the floor.

Did I fail? You betcha. Big-time. After I was able to walk again, Tinsey escorted me to the door and told me never to come back. I never did. But I chose not to see that event as a failure. Instead, it was a learner's mistake—an opportunity for growth. What did I learn? Never go behind someone's back. If you need to meet with people other than the person you're currently working with, make sure you find a valid reason for it and, if possible, engage your current contact in setting it up.

When you reframe failures as valuable learning experiences, everything changes. You stop being so hard on yourself. You quit trying to do things perfectly. You're a whole lot less stressed, which is good, because now your brain is able to think a whole lot more clearly and creatively.

Reframing failure frees you up to learn, experiment, and

grow in your capabilities. This mind-set is crucial when you're new to a job. Judging yourself too harshly in your early months gets in the way of achieving your potential.

If you're struggling, you're not failing. You just haven't learned it yet. I love that mode of thinking; it always motivates me to keep going, knowing that success is imminent.

Sometimes reframing failure is even more important when you're an experienced professional. If it's been a long time since you've been in a learning mode, you're going to feel rusty learning new information and awkward trying out new skills. Every bone in your body will want to revert to your habitual way of doing things. That would be a big mistake. If you're not continually growing in this sales environment, you're falling behind.

If you're still hung up on failing, it's time to make a decision. You can live in fear of failure and become only a fraction of the person you're meant to be. Or you can choose to reframe failure in a way that allows you to accept screwups as just a part of learning.

Failure is your route to success. Remember, if you don't choose to learn from your mistakes, you're doomed to repeat them again and again, until you either quit or finally get it. Once you reframe failure, you move forward. That's why this mind-set matters.

> Reframe failures as valuable learning experiences.

8

SET THE RIGHT GOALS

What kind of goals should you establish to ensure success? In sales, we most often set performance-based goals like "achieve 165 percent of quota" or "make $200,000." While it's admirable to strive for the stars, research shows that big goals can actually be a hindrance, especially before you've achieved a level of proficiency.

That happened to me. I once had a sales manager who insisted in January that I set an income goal for the year. He told me to really stretch by picking one that was far more than I'd ever earned before. So I did, but it didn't feel doable. My boss suggested that I break the goal down by months, weeks, and days so I could track my success. It didn't help. By the end of the first quarter, I was already behind. By the end of the second quarter, the goal was clearly unreachable. Worse yet, I felt deflated that I wouldn't reach the goal—even though I was having a decent year by all other accounts.

If performance-based goals are your primary drivers, your self-worth is tied up in achieving them. To protect your ego, you'll likely blame everything but yourself if you fail to meet your goals.

Instead, we need "getting better" goals. According to psychologist Don VandeWalle, these goals are "focused on acquiring new skills, mastering new situations and improving one's confidence." In his study, salespeople with "getting better" goal orientations actually set higher sales targets, worked harder, planned better, and achieved significantly more. Clearly, a getting-better mind-set is much more motivating than setting blue-sky performance goals.

But it takes more than that. Agile sellers have a purpose and a process that ensures they keep on getting better. In *Succeed*, Heidi Grant Halvorson expands on this concept. Her work at the Columbia Business School's Motivation Science Center shows that we also need two other types of goals:

- "Why" goals for motivation. They help us get in touch with the benefits we'll realize from achieving this goal.
- "What" goals in order to achieve our big picture. That means we need to outline, to the best of our knowledge, specifically what actions we need to take to accomplish our goal.

Recently, I heard an interview with Tiger Woods, shortly after he'd won his fourth tournament of the 2013 PGA Tour season. After a three-year drought, he'd just regained his number-one ranking. The sportscaster interviewing Woods asked him, "So how do you think you're doing?" His response: "I'm getting better."

Tiger didn't say he'd reached his goal of winning a tournament. Instead, he focused on his improvement, which included a whole slew of "what" goals. Over the years, he's analyzed every aspect of his golf game to find areas he can improve. Most recently, he's been working on perfecting his swing; it's his third major swing overhaul as a pro. He's always working on his putting too, because it's not as consistent as he wants it to be.

Why does Tiger do all this? He wants to be on top again, of course, but he knows that focusing on reaching that singular goal doesn't help him achieve it. It's getting better, incrementally, that matters. And, because he often gets a whole lot worse before he sees any improvement, he doesn't need the pressure of performance goals.

That's what agile sellers do too. Their mind-set is one of continuous improvement. They set getting-better goals. Their "why" is personal; they know what motivates them. They dissect what they're currently doing to find areas they can strengthen.

In the upcoming chapters, you'll find numerous strategies for improving your selling skills and getting up to speed quickly. You'll also find very specific actions you can take to increase your learning agility and deepen your knowledge. Make sure you set the right goals to help you along.

> Turn performance goals into getting-better goals.

Part 3

Learn New Info Quickly

So much to learn, so little time. Find out how to get
off to a fast start by quickly mastering the crucial
"must know now" information needed in your job.

9

FAST-TRACK TO PROFICIENCY

Most people never pay much attention to how they learn. Usually, when you find yourself in a new situation, you muddle through it as best you can. Yet in very short order, you're seriously overwhelmed. You actually begin to doubt if it's even feasible for you to learn it all. Does this sound familiar?

Believe it or not, for fifteen years I lived in a world of serious overwhelm, by choice. At that time, I was helping sales organizations jump-start sales of their new products and services. Companies typically brought me on board a few months prior to their launch date. In weeks, I had to learn about their new offerings, customers, marketplace, competition, and the business case for change. I also needed to understand their sales methodology, challenges, and obstacles to success.

It was always tough to get the information I needed from my clients. Sometimes they gave me nothing. Other times I wasted tons of time sorting through piles of unrelated content trying to find the hidden gems. I spent untold hours talking to well-intentioned people who rambled on and on about seemingly irrelevant topics in the name of information gathering.

Once I'd digested everything I needed to know, I then had to quickly develop sales playbooks that included ideal prospect definitions, effective value propositions, prospecting scripts, initial meeting plans, presentation slides, and other tools to help salespeople get up to speed quickly. When that was done, I developed a fully customized training program for my clients' sales teams.

To say it was a lot to learn in a short period is a gross understatement. At first, I did about three launches per year. Before long, I was doing ten to twelve annually. To further complicate the situation, at least 60 percent of the client launches were in markets with which I was totally unfamiliar. During those years, I probably sold more products and services into different market segments than any other human being in the entire world. Strike that; I mean galaxy.

There were times when I wondered if I'd ever be able to make sense of it all. But over time, I became an agile learner with a rock-solid process that enabled me to swoop into any company, quickly find the info I needed, and turn it into usable sales tools and training. Ultimately, what made this impossible task possible were two things: 1) I discovered what I needed to learn; and 2) I learned how to learn it quickly.

In sales, we don't have the luxury of time; we're expected to produce results right away. Focusing on rapid learning strategies helps us quickly assimilate new knowledge and develop new skills. That's what this section is all about, acquiring a baseline of knowledge. After all, you need to know what you're selling and to whom before you actually start.

> Knowing what to learn and how to learn is essential for success.

10

LEVERAGE RAPID LEARNING

Learning agility is an acquired skill. Most people don't know that; they think either they're good at picking things up quickly or they're bad at it. We often view ourselves simply as receptacles of information that our company thinks we need to know. With this belief, we stumble along haphazardly, not knowing we can control the unending flow of data. Because we're so seldom in situations where we have so much to learn, we may not even know that a highly effective learning process actually exists.

I learned how to learn because my consulting job demanded it. My experience, though, was all through trial and error. I had no guidance on the best ways to learn. But over the past few decades, there's been a growing body of research into how our brain works. We now know so much more about how our brain understands, remembers, decides, inhibits, analyzes, prioritizes, and creates information. In the upcoming chapters, you'll discover how these neuroscience findings can be applied through practical, hands-on tips and techniques for jump-starting your knowledge acquisition.

The six rapid learning strategies we'll focus on can be applied to virtually anything at which you'd like to become proficient. You can use these techniques to learn how to fly a plane, develop a Web site, or speak a different language. Your prior knowledge and experience affect your starting point but do not alter the need for these strategies. Here's a quick overview of the six strategies:

Chunking. Breaking big subjects down into smaller, more digestible chunks is always your first task in rapid learning. Otherwise, the assignment is simply too overwhelming. Your brain loves structure. It files all new knowledge into mental folders, wherever it thinks is the best fit. By creating the specific folders yourself, you significantly increase your recall and retention. You also free up processing power for more complex mental tasks (such as planning an account strategy).

Sequencing. After you've broken the subject or skill set down into discrete chunks, you have to determine what you need to learn first, and what comes after that. Most people don't take control of this step; they just take in the information as it's being delivered. But if things aren't learned in the right order, they often don't make sense.

Connecting. Linking new skills and information to something you already know is a great way to expedite learning and retention. For example, you might reflect on how your new job is similar to previous positions. Leveraging a connection strategy is one of the fastest ways to grasp new concepts because you already have mental folders in which you can file new learning.

Dumping. Your brain gets bogged down easily. The more it has to remember, the worse it works. The key to remembering a deluge of information is getting what you learn out of your head and into a place where you can look at it later. This isn't a fancy strategy but it is a highly functional one because it frees up brain space for learning more.

Practicing. Any time you need to learn a skill, deliberate practice is essential. When it comes to sales, the way to practice is through role-playing. Many sellers ignore this critical strategy, yet it's only by trying new things in semi–real time that you know if you're ready for prime time. Practicing is a test with a built-in feedback loop. Further, each time you practice a new skill, it cements the new behaviors more firmly in place.

Prioritizing. Your brain is incapable of doing two functions simultaneously. Contrary to popular belief, multitasking isn't a good way to get many things done at once. It actually causes serious degradation of the brain's processing power. To harness your most effective thinking, decide which activities are most important at the beginning of each day and then focus on one activity at a time, to the exclusion of all others.

In the upcoming chapters, you'll find numerous ways to apply each of these learning strategies to your sales job. You'll also find tools to help you slash your path to proficiency.

> To learn faster, chunk, sequence, connect, dump, practice, and prioritize.

11

MAP THE TERRAIN

When I did sales coaching a few years back, I worked with a sales rep named Antonio. When we met, he was pretty discouraged with his sales success. He had recently started working for a new company in the full-services marketing industry, but was already seriously questioning if he had made a bad decision in taking the job.

Aside from a half-day orientation, Antonio didn't receive any structured sales training from his company. Instead, he was passed from one person in the company to the next. Each was expected to give Antonio a download of everything he needed to know about his or her area of expertise. Antonio was soon drowning in an ocean of disconnected information. His brain was in major overload trying to remember it all, much less make sense of it.

I'm sure you've felt overloaded by information yourself. When there's so much to learn, you often don't know where to begin. Even if your company has a decent onboarding program, it can be overwhelming. You're often on your own way too soon, with-

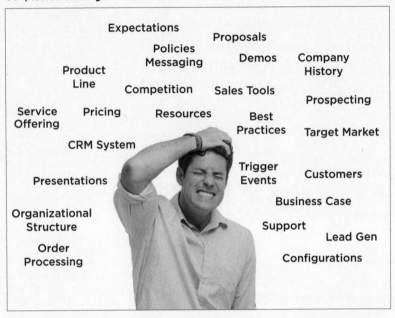

out good direction on how to use all the material you've been exposed to. When I did product launches, I felt overwhelmed on every single project I worked on. My head was spinning. Your poor little brain can retain only so much before it shouts, "Stop! I can't take any more!"

I assured Antonio that his feelings of not catching on were totally normal. To get through it, however, he needed to take control of his own learning. Enough of that passive sponge behavior and trying to absorb all the information at once. That would be an impossible task, given that his brain was in full rebellion.

To get himself on a better path for strategically learning what he needed to know, the first thing Antonio needed to do was to dump, dump, dump. I had him start by writing down everything he thought he needed to learn. His endless list included items such as knowing all the details about the company's different services, understanding its unique methodology, what differentiated it from competitors, how to price things, how to get meetings, and more.

Next, I asked Antonio to write down the info that people had already told him. This long list included practices such as how to use the CRM system and fill out expense reports, what went into a proposal, customer projects that were currently in process, insurance policy info, what makes a good presentation, and whom to go to for help.

Getting everything out of his head and down on paper helped. Looking at the slew of information on his list, Antonio could see why he was overwhelmed and couldn't remember things—it was just too much. Once the swirling stopped, he could now focus on creating order out of this chaos.

Next we turned to chunking. According to David Rock, author of *Your Brain at Work*, research shows that four is the maximum number of chunks our brain can optimally process for a given set of information. During my product launch consulting days, I'd discovered that the best chunks for salespeople to use were: company, products/services, customers, and sales. Within each of these chunks are subchunks for each of the primary subsets.

In order to remember and retain the information as best he could, Antonio had to divide and file the information into four separate categories. To help him start his sorting process, I showed him the mind map (on the next page) that I'd used for years on all my product launch projects.

These four chunks, as well as their subchunks, cover almost everything you need to learn to get up to speed quickly in your new sales position. And that's the first step—knowing what you need to learn.

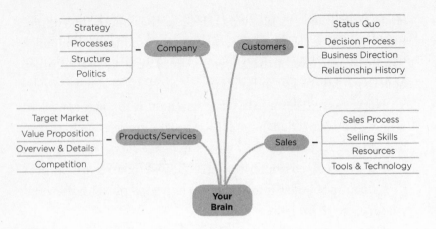

Once you've come up with these chunks, what do you do with them? Start by creating mental storage "folders" for each of them—with very specific names such as Target Market, Prospecting Strategies, or CRM System.

More than that, you also need physical or virtual folders for all relevant resources you're given or discovering in your learning quest. This seemingly simple action is actually a powerful strategy for recalling what you've learned at the moment in time when you need to use that information. Keep your folders and mind maps visible. They can be used almost like a checklist to help you keep track of what you've already learned and what you still need to tackle.

Now, back to Antonio. Once he broke his new job's requirements into chunks, he felt immediate relief. Things weren't quite as chaotic as he had feared. Once he began applying the learning strategies to the information he had collected, he was able to recall things more quickly, figure out what he already knew, and decide where to focus next.

Chunking is only the start of the rapid learning process. Af-

ter establishing this learning repository, your next job is to figure out the sequence of learning, how much you'll need to know
in each area, and the priorities of what you still need to learn.
With only a finite amount of time to get up to speed, it's crucial
to make these decisions correctly.

> Chunking strategies minimize mental
> chaos and increase recall.

12

TAKE THE DEEP DIVE

The first few months of any position are guaranteed to require nonstop learning. I know you'd love to cram everything into your head during that time, but unless you come from a very similar job, it may not be possible. According to sales management expert Lee Salz, it takes a minimum of eight months for new salespeople to perform at the same level as their tenured colleagues—even if they're experienced sellers.

Because it's nearly an impossibility to be an overnight expert, you need to set a different goal for yourself. What should you shoot for?

Situational credibility in thirty days. This means that in just one month, you'll have a working knowledge of what's most important to your prospects and customers. That will enable you to:

- Have a decent conversation with prospects without sounding like a novice.
- Ask insightful questions that position you as a credible resource.

- Demonstrate your knowledge of their issues, challenges, objectives, and more.

To achieve situational credibility in thirty days, you need to take a deep dive. By that, I mean you're going to focus intensely on learning as much as you can right away. According to DDI*, a leading talent management firm, getting off to a strong start is crucial. If people don't sense progress within thirty days, they lose confidence, begin to dislike their jobs, and start pulling back and dwelling on the negatives. Just like that, they're looking for another job. It's a bad cycle to get caught in.

That's why it's smart to expedite your path to proficiency. The thirty-day deep dive, while intense, offers huge payback. Here are some tips to help you make the most of this time.

Set yourself up for learning. Quite simply, be prepared to learn. You wouldn't go to your first day of class without a notebook and a pen, and you should be similarly ready to learn in a new role. You're going to be taking lots of notes in the upcoming weeks, so have some notepads handy. I'd also suggest getting a bunch of folders so that you can immediately categorize and sort information about products, services, markets, buyers, and decision processes as you learn it. Otherwise, the piles accumulate and you'll never find what you need when you need it. If you prefer to organize online, get yourself set up there too—there are useful online organizational tools available. You can use the same folder labels. Same concept, just different media.

Use your grace period. No one expects you to know everything when you're new to a job or account. Most of your

---

* William C. Byham, Ph.D., chairman and CEO of Development Dimensions International (DDI), *Strong Start to Job Success*, white paper, www.boyden.uk.com/mediafiles/attachments/1375.pdf.

bosses and colleagues are ready to help answer questions you may have, so don't let your ego get in the way of learning. Keep a running list of questions you need answered.

Update the boss regularly. Your employer may have turned you loose to learn on your own. Even so, regularly sharing what you've recently learned shows him or her that you take your professional development seriously. Your boss will be thoroughly impressed with the initiative you're taking to get up to speed quickly. Share what you're planning for the upcoming week. Bring your calendar along to show how you're using your time. You may not think this matters, but it does. Invariably, you'll get extra support when you need it.

Know how you learn best. Everyone has his or her own learning style preference. Personally, I like to read; I'm a visual learner. You may prefer to learn by listening or by physically engaging with the new content. What matters is that you find a way that works best for you.

Finally, be kind to yourself. In times of deep dive, you can be your own worst enemy. Keep focusing on "getting better" goals. Make sure you take a few moments now and then to reflect on how much you've already learned. Sometimes you'll even impress yourself.

Next, we'll focus on the first step in this thirty-day deep dive, which will expedite your learning exponentially in your new sales position.

> Use the thirty-day deep dive to develop situational credibility.

13

FOCUS ON "NEED TO KNOWS"

Recently I listened to Tim Ferriss, author of *The 4-Hour Work-week*, speak about rapid learning. He's an expert at mastering new subjects in an unbelievably short period of time. His process involves breaking new info down into discrete chunks, then searching for the "minimum effective dose." The goal is to find the least amount of work needed to produce outstanding results fast.

This strategy works with sales too. To get up to speed quickly in your new sales role, you don't need to learn everything at once. Besides, it's insanely counterproductive; there's no way that it's humanly possible to remember it all. In order to become proficient, however, you should immediately focus on finding the "minimum effective dose."

After doing numerous launch projects, I realized that certain information was vital for jump-starting sales success for any client. Without this "need to know" information, it was difficult to get new prospects into the pipeline or hold productive conversations with them.

I also discovered that directing this "need to know"

information-gathering process was crucial. Otherwise, people would inundate me with facts and figures they felt were important but that really didn't matter in the short term. Their eagerness to share their knowledge actually had negative effects and bogged down my brain. If you're in that situation now, tell your "teacher" that while you appreciate all his or her help, your brain has capacity limitations and you'd be better off waiting until later to learn all of that information. Say it with a smile. Then, very graciously, take control of your own learning process.

Below are the questions to use in differentiating between what you need to learn now and what can wait. I've used these guiding questions over and over—and they work for separating essential information from the nonessential. You may need to talk to a few different people to get the answers you need, but the payback is worth it. You'll be more productive, much faster.

Start with the big picture. Research shows your brain needs a conceptual overview before it can take in the details. Ask your boss and coworkers these questions:

- Can you give me an overview of the primary products or services I'll be selling?
- What's the target market for these offerings? Why are they a good fit?
- Without going into detail, how do they help these customers/companies? What outcomes do they get?

These questions will give you the overall framework of what you're selling, to whom, and why it matters.

Determine your priorities. Separating the "need to know" from the "nice to know" is my favorite step because it immediately simplifies your life. Again, check with your boss and colleagues to help determine your priorities. Dig into the "whys" of their responses too, so you understand their rationale.

- Which of our products and services are key to our company's success this year?
- Which of our products/services are the best door openers?
- If I could sell only one of our products/services this year, which would it be?
- Which of our products/services are our existing customers most interested in?
- Do we have any products/services that aren't really all that popular?
- If we're selling into multiple industries, where is the best place to start?
- Which market segments present the best opportunities right now?
- Who are the most influential people involved in the decision-making process?
- What factors, if any (such as time of year), impact product/service sales?

At this point, you've identified the "minimum effective dose." Ignore nonessential learning for now. Your job, at this moment, is to learn as much as you can about the "need to knows."

For additional insight, make sure to ask: "Can you give me an example?" The more detailed examples you get, the better. Real-life scenarios stick in your brain better than generalities.

Speaking of examples, remember Antonio from chapter 11? I told you earlier that he was selling for a full-services marketing agency. His company prided itself on being a "marketing department in a box," offering services including branding, marketing automation, lead generation, scalable online training, and more, to clients from a wide variety of industries.

No wonder Antonio's head was spinning. Based on my suggestion, he talked to his boss about feeling overwhelmed with all he had to learn. Speaking up was a crucial first step for Antonio, and, as it turns out, his boss had no idea he was struggling. (Note: Your boss is not a mind reader. You need to speak up when you're floundering, especially at the start, so he or she can help you.) To assist Antonio in making sense of his assignment, they discussed the questions I outlined above.

Based on their conversation, the boss decided that Antonio would spend all his time in the next three months selling lead generation services to the technology sector. Getting more high-quality leads in the door was a hot issue with these companies, so setting up initial meetings was much easier.

Now, instead of having to know everything about his company's many marketing services, Antonio could focus on a niche area. He took a deep dive into this specific market segment. Using the above questions with his boss and colleagues, he homed in even more on "need to know" information. Before long, Antonio had developed enough situational credibility that he was able to have productive conversations with his prospects.

The strategy of focusing on "need to knows" and minimum effective doses worked. Antonio developed proficiency in one area, which enabled him to win some deals fairly quickly. With this success under his belt, it was much easier for him to expand into other market segments and to sell a wider variety of services.

The key is to focus on only the crucial information at the start. More than anything else, it gives you something to build on. While you may not be able to create such a finite segment as Antonio did, you can certainly sequence your learning so the most valuable information comes first. Ask the right questions, determine your priorities, and focus on learning everything you can about them.

Focus initial learning on crucial
"need to know" info.

14

LEARN THE LINGO

This one's a quick tip. When you begin digging into any new environment, you'll quickly discover that every company speaks its own language. If you're not familiar with it, it can sound like an alien tongue. Colleagues talk about things like partition pruning, run rates, and human capital analytics, sprinkling acronyms like DBA, B2B, and BPO throughout their conversation. They may frequently use terms like TCO, EBITDA, and DSOs too.

After selling for many years as well as working on so many new product launches, I've discovered how crucial it is to learn the lingo quickly.

Starting on day one, create your own dictionary. Any time you hear a new word or phrase, jot it down immediately. Then, when you get time, ask someone in the company to define it for you. Make sure you get *precise* definitions too, or you'll still be floundering.

Here are the categories you'll want to include in your personalized dictionary:

- Company: any terms or acronyms that are specific to your organization. They could cover a variety of topics including your products or services, financing options, or compensation programs.
- Industry: broader terms that would be recognizable to a wider range of people working in your industry. These words may be used to describe processes, trends, systems, or methodologies. Your customers expect you to know this information.
- Financial: any financial terminology needed to help your prospects determine if a change from the status quo is in their best interest. It's imperative to know your prospects' key financial drivers.
- Other: a catchall group for those words, phrases, idioms, or acronyms that don't fit anywhere else. I'll never forget the time my sales manager told me that I needed to "get in bed with my prospects." Upon clarification, I discovered it wasn't meant literally.

Creating a personalized dictionary speeds up your retention, enables you to grasp new concepts faster, and increases your conversational fluency. It also helps you "join the club" of your new colleagues and clients.

What's the best format for your dictionary? Whatever works best for you. You can write it down, create mind maps, develop flash cards, make a spreadsheet, or keep it online. Personally I like to keep things on one sheet because then everything is together. The key is ease and accessibility.

Whenever you're stumped by a word or phrase, risk asking the stupid question: "What does that mean?" Looking clueless for a minute is a whole lot better than being clueless for a lifetime.

> Learning the lingo deepens
> understanding and credibility.

15

BUILD ON BUYER INSIGHTS

Of all the things I've discovered during my years in sales, this topic is one of the most crucial to sales success. Given the chance, I'd step on the highest sales podium in the world and shout out, "Understanding *who* you're selling to is far more important than *what* you're selling!"

People, not organizations, make decisions. The more you know about what makes your buyers tick, the better off you'll be. Without a doubt, this is "need to know" now information.

Unfortunately, many companies don't realize the primacy of this point. They spend hours and days when you're new explaining all the gory details of their products and services. Yet when you ask about decision makers, they don't have a lot of good information to give you. Please don't let that stop your quest for knowledge. This is too vital to your sales success. Instead, pursue this information with a vengeance on your own.

Start by finding out who is involved in making decisions. Is it the chief marketing officer, VP of communications, the trade show director—or all three? In bigger companies today, committees of five to seven people often make buying decisions. While all players are important to you, some have more clout than others. Find out who's a power player so you can target your learning.

Once you nail down the positions, you need to understand their roles and responsibilities, objectives, motivations, status quo, and challenges. This essential info helps you:

- Craft relevant, enticing messages.
- Plan customer-engaging meetings.
- Help people make the right decisions.
- Differentiate yourself from competitors.

It's easy to get lost in irrelevant information. That's why I developed a tool—the Buyer's Matrix—to keep me on track. This worksheet, essentially a snapshot of what's most important to our key decision makers, enables me to quickly get to the core of what really matters to the buyer, in record time. I've used it for years on product launches and to grow my own business. I also use it when doing sales training.

It can be a real challenge to complete this Buyer's Matrix. Often in my workshops, even experienced sellers are stumped by some of the questions. But the smart ones quickly realize that if they find out the answers, they'll be in a much stronger position.

You may have to interview multiple people in your organization to get the complete picture. Consider talking to your leadership team, colleagues, marketing, or any customer-interfacing people to gather their insights and flesh out the matrix.

Another great resource for filling out the Buyer's Matrix is LinkedIn. If you know people who currently hold any of these

BUYER'S MATRIX

Position _____

Roles/Responsibilities: *What are they in charge of or expected to manage?*

Business Objectives and Metrics: *What do they want to achieve? How do they measure success? How are they evaluated?*

Strategic Initiatives: *What likely strategies and initiatives are in place to help them achieve their objectives?*

Internal Challenges: *What likely issues does the organization face that could prevent/hinder goal achievement?*

External Challenges: *What external factors or industry trends might make it more difficult to reach their objectives?*

Primary Interfaces: *Who do they frequently interact with (e.g., peers, subordinates, superiors, and external resources)?*

Status Quo: *What's their status quo relative to your product or service?*

Change Drivers: *What would cause them to change from what they're currently doing?*

Change Inhibitors: *What would cause them to stay with the status quo, even if they're unhappy?*

buying roles, read their profile summaries and job descriptions to learn more about their responsibilities, accomplishments, and initiatives. You can use advanced search to identify people who hold these positions and then dig in. Finally, you can ask your prospects themselves to answer any outstanding questions on the matrix. If they feel that you're sincerely interested, they'll often share it with you.

This Buyer's Matrix exercise goes a long way in developing your situational credibility. Gathering these insights early in your new position enables you to better serve your prospects at the same time you increase your sales.

Next, we'll take a quick look at your prospect's status quo. Again, this is crucial "need to know" info that speeds you along on your pathway to proficiency.

> Use the Buyer's Matrix to ensure in-depth knowledge about key decision makers.

BONUS: Download a free Buyer's Matrix sample and template here: www.agilesellingbook.com.

16

EMBRACE THE STATUS QUO

If you don't know how your prospects are handling things today—without your product or service—selling is infinitely harder. Yet over and over again, companies fail to share this invaluable information with their salespeople. Why do they make this sales-derailing mistake? Because they don't realize just how much sellers need it.

The truth is, the status quo is your biggest competitor. Your prospects don't want to change how they're doing things. It takes time and energy they don't have. Don't forget, their brains are overloaded too. According to research from the Sales Benchmark Index, 60 percent of all forecasted opportunities are lost to "no decision."

Ouch! And many of those lost opportunities were from good prospects who were pretty far along in the sales process. That's why it's imperative that you learn about their status quo early on. Every single day, you're up against it. Unless you really understand how prospects address their needs right now, it's difficult to put together a good rationale for change.

Begin by identifying which of the three most common status quo scenarios you'll most likely run into with the products or services you'll be selling. To get started, ask your colleagues this one question: "How do our targeted prospects do things without us?" Find out if they're using competitors, and if so, which ones. If you're in the services business, find out if a company's internal resources may already be doing the work you provide.

Once you've found the most common status quos, you want to understand them on a deeper level. Ask your colleagues these questions to gain invaluable insights into why a company would change:

- What problems might they be encountering with their current way of doing things?
- How do these problems impact efficiencies? Costs? Revenue? Other departments?
- What effect does this status quo have on achieving their objectives?
- What's the business case for making a change?
- What issues might arise if they're doing it themselves?

Ask these questions in your first thirty days. Your goal is to figure out the potential pitfalls of each of the primary status quos. Use whatever resources are available to you to get this information. Research online. Listen to industry experts.

Knowing this information makes a big difference. When I started selling technology, many of my prospects used an older office automation system from one particular vendor. Because I didn't understand it very well, they could easily brush me off, telling me everything was fine with their current system. After a few too many failures, I took a deep dive and immersed myself in learning as much as I could about the existing system's capabilities and how they affected workflow. Before long, I uncovered major inefficiencies that actually added to the companies' labor costs. Knowing this invaluable info helped me open doors and close many sales.

Lee, a salesperson I'd worked with when he sold staffing services, faced a very different challenge when he started selling aircraft and aviation insurance. All his prospects had a current provider. For the most part, they just kept renewing their policies without even thinking. To make matters worse, people didn't want to waste time meeting with Lee to learn about what his company could do for them.

Lee desperately needed to find some reason for prospects to consider looking at a different option. He started by exploring the following questions:

- What are they already buying from my competitors?
- What do we offer that they might not have right now?
- What might my competitors have overlooked when they initially sold this policy?
- Have any changes occurred that could get them to rethink their original decision?

In doing this analysis, Lee uncovered a regulatory change in aviation insurance that could potentially have an impact on how his prospects did business. He also realized that companies that hadn't changed their insurers for a while were potentially missing important areas of coverage. Now, instead of contacting prospects about their general insurance needs, Lee focused on the issues he'd uncovered. As a result, he was able to set up many more conversations by showing prospects how the status quo had actually changed.

Immerse yourself in the status quo. Search for its weaknesses, shortcomings, and gaps. Once you have a working knowledge of your biggest competitor—the status quo—you'll be able to have more intelligent conversations with your prospects.

> Become an expert on your biggest competitor—the status quo.

17

REVERSE ENGINEER THE BUSINESS CASE

I f you don't understand the real value you bring to customers, you've got a tough sales assignment ahead of you. Unfortunately, when you're new in a position or when new products are launched, you're often handed a whole bunch of self-serving pabulum from marketing that touts how great your stuff is. You may even be told that if you share these glowing benefits with your prospects, they'll stand in line to buy from you.

This approach does not work. Not one little bit. According to the Edelman Trust Barometer, only 8 percent of people trust what companies say about themselves.

To successfully sell, you need to be able to clearly articulate your value proposition. Your value proposition is "need to know" information that answers the question, "Why should your prospects change from the status quo—especially after they've been living with an imperfect one for years?" This answer is your business case for change. The stronger it is, the more likely your prospects will take action.

Many companies fail to arm their sellers with a strong business case. They still believe that their products or services sell themselves. I don't. That's why, when I was doing launches, I found it necessary to reverse engineer virtually every piece of marketing collateral that my client was planning to use. I still do it today because it's one of the fastest ways I know to get a handle on the business case for change.

Recently, I ran a workshop for a firm that sells cable rejuvenation technology to power companies. To say I'm a novice in this area is a major understatement. I've never worked with utilities, so I'm clueless about their products, and I didn't know their sales process. Yet I had to get up to speed quickly in order to customize a workshop with their sales team.

Here's how I tackled reverse engineering their business case. First, I went to the company's Web site and printed out high-level product descriptions so I could get a general overview of their offering. Next, I poked around their resources page to find any white papers, videos, e-books, or audios that addressed any of their customers' key challenges. (Note: If your company lacks good content, check out competitive sites. They can be a gold mine.)

Then I requested two specific types of materials from the VP of sales: recent case studies and presentation slides that their salespeople used early in the sales process. After I collected all of this material, I dug in and began reading. Mostly I saw what I usually do: lots of boring descriptions about their stuff and their company. There was also the obligatory puffery and tired buzzwords (for example, "passion for excellence," "state-of-the-art") that marketers feel compelled to use. I skipped right over that. I was on a mission to figure out the *change rationale*—why people would spend tons of money with them when their current situation was tolerable.

As I reviewed the content, phrases like "increased reliability" and "reduced failure rates" popped out at me because of their repeated use. Clearly, they were important. But from a sales perspective, they were also undeveloped. The business case for change wasn't readily apparent.

Once I figured out where to focus, I dug into finding out what was really behind those benefit statements. I called the sales VP and asked him a series of questions, including:

- When cables fail, what happens?
- What are the direct costs to fix?
- What are the indirect costs? Opportunity costs?
- Who/what else is affected? What happens then?
- Why wouldn't they have changed earlier?

By asking these questions, I got a better picture of the buyers' environment, their challenges, and the total cost of continuing with the status quo. In fact, there were compelling financial reasons for the prospects to take immediate action to rejuvenate their cables. During the workshop, using the information from the reverse engineering exercise, I helped the salespeople see the true value of what they were selling as well as how to leverage it to open more doors and close more sales.

Reverse engineering is a good way to get clear on your business case. When you do this, you truly "get" why people change. Understanding this is so important that next I'm going to show you another way to gather this vital data.

> Use reverse engineering to clearly articulate the business case.

BONUS: Download my free Value Proposition Tool Kit here: www.agilesellingbook.com.

18

SINK INTO STORIES

What's the best way to cement everything you've learned so far into your already overloaded brain? With stories.

Your brain loves stories—it remembers narratives a gazillion times longer than a bunch of disparate facts. What you need are rich, meaty stories that give you a deep understanding of your product or service's value in the context of your customer's world.

Let me give you an example. After eleven years in advertising, Matt was excited about his new position at a consulting firm. He had lots to learn as the company's proprietary innovation methodology involved multiple steps. Matt spent his first few months immersed in understanding the practice, even observing numerous sessions. He thought he got it.

However, when he tried to explain this methodology to his prospects, they didn't get it. Worse yet, they yawned at his detailed explanations. Nothing he said piqued their curiosity or induced them to open their wallets. As you might imagine, he was seriously frustrated when he contacted me.

Turns out, Matt was telling the wrong story. His focus had been on his own company's story. He was totally missing the one that mattered—the client's story. Matt really didn't understand the business value his company provided. I told him that it was time to find out from his colleagues why their clients thought it was worth spending so much money with them.

One particular story, about a large food manufacturer, really helped him understand the business case. The marketers at this big company were faced with a real dilemma. Research showed that if children didn't develop a taste for their product before the age of five, they'd never eat it. Yet fewer and fewer mothers bought it for their kids. Everyone at this company had an opinion about what would work best, but they were polarized and unable to move forward. The whole company knew, though, that if they didn't come up with a hot new product idea soon, they'd lose a generation of customers.

That's where Matt's firm came in, pulling together a multiday innovation session to address this issue. To kick it off, they brought in a group of young moms whom they'd previously trained in creative brainstorming. In their day together, Matt's colleagues led these women through numerous activities to come up with a boatload of new product ideas. Then, for the next two days, their firm facilitated sessions with the marketers to pick the product with the greatest potential.

The net result of these sessions was that Matt's company helped their client identify a product idea that everyone supported wholeheartedly. Better yet, it turned into a blockbuster success. First-year sales were far better than projected, allowing them to recapture a market segment they were previously losing.

When Matt heard this story from his colleagues, he finally

understood why prospects would pay so much for his company's services. It gave him the much-needed confidence in his sales initiatives.

Matt now had a story he could share with potential clients. They could all relate to the pressure to come up with break-through products, the stress of dealing with divergent opinions, and the difficulty of coming to an agreement on a new direction. Moreover, the outcome of the story echoed what his potential clients were hoping to achieve. Best of all, when Matt told this story, the clients—not his company—were the heroes. His prospects loved it.

Get the picture? Stories are important. That's why I shared Matt's with you, so you'd see how it works. Every company has stories but they're often hidden and need to be pulled out.

Recently, I did a workshop with a growing technology firm that had doubled its sales force in the previous year. However, when you combined the fresh faces with the company's natural attrition rate, not too many salespeople working there knew the client stories anymore. We took some time during the session to share these important narratives so that the rookies could truly understand the value of their technology from the customer's perspective.

Seek out stories. Find out about the issues that caused clients to take action. Learn how your company helped. Most important, find out what difference it made. When you know the difference you make, selling is much easier.

Identify stories that pique buyers' curiosity and move them to action.

19

INTERVIEW CUSTOMERS

Let's keep talking about stories for one more chapter. They're that important.

One of the best things you can do to learn why people buy your products or services is to interview your own customers. Don't be shy about this. You'll be amazed at what you can learn and just how valuable it can be in your sales initiatives.

But whom do you interview? After all, you're new in this job and may not have your own customers yet. I strongly suggest you talk to people who have decided to work with your company in the past six to twelve months. Long-term customers may love your company to death, but they don't make for high-value interviews since they have no recent basis of comparison. You are their status quo.

Your most recent customers, however, know what life was like under the previous status quo. They can tell you how things have changed since their relationship with your company began. They may also be able to give you quantifiable business results that you'll be able to use in your prospecting efforts.

Start by picking out a few customers in your territory that

you'd like to interview. Tell them that you're following up to find out if they're getting the results they'd anticipated when they decided to work with your company. Ask if they'd be willing to spare a few minutes to answer questions about this topic. Quite often, they're willing to help you out. (Be aware that you may occasionally run into an unhappy customer. If so, listen carefully to their issues and don't be defensive. Find out what you can do to help.)

If the customer agrees to a short conversation, I'd suggest conducting this interview via phone. It's more efficient. Believe it or not, people tell you a whole lot more over the phone than if you're face-to-face. And don't waste your time trying to do it via e-mail or online surveys; the response rate is low and the quality of info is poor.

Make sure you plan your questions ahead of time. Otherwise, the conversation can wander all over the place and the answers you get won't be helpful. Consider recording your interview too, so that you can listen to it again for insights you might have missed the first time.

To give you an idea of what one of these interviews might look like, I've included a snippet of one of these conversations below between Sarah and a client. Sarah was an inside sales rep, hired to sell software over the phone. She was really struggling in the new job. Her boss instructed her to emphasize the software's wonderful features and capabilities, but prospects didn't seem to be impressed. They kept telling Sarah everything was fine with their current technology.

When I asked Sarah to tell me the business case for using her company's software, she had trouble clearly articulating it. I knew right away that it was a root-cause problem that was negatively impacting all her interactions with potential buyers.

I had Sarah reach out to a fairly recent customer. Before they talked, she spent time mapping out the questions that she wanted to ask. When they connected, she thanked the client for his time and reiterated her desire to learn more about how her software had affected his department. Then she began to ask him questions.

SARAH: Ethan, how's our application helping in your development area?

ETHAN: It was a real hassle to make changes without it, so we're getting lots more done. Plus, we can copy actual customers into our environment so it's saving us lots of time there too.

SARAH: So how much time do you think it's saving you?

ETHAN: I'd say at least a total day on many projects. But when we have problems, sometimes it's saved us up to forty hours for the life cycle of the client.

SARAH: Wow. That's a lot of time savings. Does that mean you're getting through your backlog faster?

ETHAN: Absolutely. Programmers can keep working on the same thing without having to jump back and forth. We get lots more done without the interruptions.

SARAH: Are you getting the results you'd hoped for when you decided to get it?

ETHAN: Yes. I'd say we've saved at least $15,000 in labor costs this year.

SARAH: Mmm. Impressive. Is your company growing too?

ETHAN: We're up about 13 percent over last year.

SARAH: Have you added lots of additional staff to handle the workload?

ETHAN: No. Just an intern. Mostly we've handled it with our

current staff. I hadn't thought of that before. In the past, we would have added at least one full-time person to keep up with things.

SARAH: I appreciate your insights. You've really helped me understand our value better.

Sarah contacted me immediately after that call. "I get it," she said excitedly. "Now I know why people buy our stuff." From that day, she changed her approach. Instead of talking to prospects about the technology and how great it was, she focused instead on what the product could do for them: save time, shrink their backlogs, and reduce labor costs. Sarah's prospects were immediately interested once she focused on what they really cared about, and her sales jumped significantly.

Knowing the difference you make in your customers' lives is essential for selling. When you're talking to prospects, it helps you position your offering. You can also ask better questions, challenge brush-offs more successfully, and build a case for change.

Don't just stop after you've interviewed one customer. In your first few months, the more people you interview, the faster you'll get up to speed. Also, consider interviewing multiple people within an organization; everyone involved in the decision process has a different perspective. Digging out these additional insights enables you to customize your message for the various buyers and increase its effectiveness.

> Interview customers to find out the
> real difference you make.

DEFINE THE BUYER'S JOURNEY

If I've heard it once, I've heard it a thousand times. When I ask salespeople about their objective for an upcoming meeting, invariably I hear, "To get a sale!" Bad answer. That only works if you're involved in a one-call sale. Most of the time, it takes multiple conversations with multiple people to get their business. Today's buyers are risk averse. If they change, they want to make sure it's the right decision.

Each stage of the buyer's journey is very distinct and requires you to use very different skills and strategies. We've already talked about where the journey starts—with the status quo. But what comes next? Typically, I find that buyers make four primary decisions.

Your challenge is to identify the specific steps that your prospects go through, from the moment their curiosity is piqued or their priorities change. You'll find that the process is often very similar from one company to the next.

For example, here's how Natalie, a digital marketing man-

1ST DECISION: ALLOW ACCESS	2ND DECISION: INITIATE CHANGE	3RD DECISION: SELECT RESOURCES	4TH DECISION EXPAND RELATIONSHIPS
Buyers are reasonably happy with the status quo—until something either piques their curiosity or changes their priorities.	Buyers are interested in learning more. They research, they meet, they discuss. The key question they ask is: Does it make sense to change from the status quo?	Buyers educate themselves on options, get proposals, meet vendors, validate ROI. Their key question is: What's the best decision for us?	Buyers evaluate satisfaction with the initial decision and relationship. Their key question is: Should we do more work with them?

ager and buyer, answers the question "What's the process for making decisions in your company?"

If you are a salesperson who contacted me from out of the blue and your message interested me, I'd go to your Web site first to check things out. If you looked like a credible company that potentially could help us, I'd agree to a short conversation. If I liked what I heard, I'd talk to my VP of marketing and lead gen specialist to share what I'd learned and bounce some ideas off them. If they were interested in learning more about your product/service, I'd want to get them on the phone with you to find out a bit more.

After that, we'd probably have some internal meetings to discuss if changing from the status quo would be a viable option. At that point, we'd probably get some other people in the company involved who are more directly involved with the issue. We'd want to meet with some of your staff too. Concurrently, we'd also be researching online how other companies handle the issues we're facing.

Our next step would be to conduct a financial analysis to assess the business case for a change. If it looked good, we'd present the results to the CFO, hoping for a go-ahead. If we got her approval, we would then go online to research other options so we can compare your offers with your competitors'. We'd check with some forums we belong to regarding their thoughts of good companies to work with.

After this, we'd invite a few companies to present a proposal. Of course, that means we have to set up meetings with all of them and answer their questions. It seems like this process never ends. Then everyone comes back with a presentation and proposal. Usually one company stands above the others. They seem to "get us" better than everyone else. If their price is competitive, we usually go with them. But first, we put them through the wringer as we try to negotiate better terms and pricing.

Finally, we'd make our selection and get started with our new product/service. But even then, it's not over. We need to evaluate the results we get to determine if it makes sense to do more business with your company.

Phew! As you can see, the buyer's journey isn't easy. Neither is your job. When you're selling it's crucial that you align with your buyer's journey. The best way to know how this journey unfolds is to map it all out—visually, on a sheet of paper or by turning it into a graphic on your computer. Keep this map in front of you until you know it by heart.

Whenever you're talking to prospects, try asking the following questions to gain even greater insight into their buying journey:

- What piques your curiosity and gets you to even consider a change?
- Who are the people who need to be involved in decisions like this?
- How do you determine if a product or service makes good business sense for your company?
- How do you decide which resource is best for you?
- What are the most challenging parts of this decision process? Why?
- What does it take to get a contract for something like this approved?

Become an expert on your buyer's journey. Knowing where you stand in the journey will help you decide which strategies to use and when.

> Know your buyer's journey
> so you can align with it.

21

CREATE CHEAT SHEETS

The problem with learning too much too quickly is that it's easy to forget things. You can't trust your memory; unless you pay rapt attention to what you're learning, it can evaporate in no time. Just think of how quickly you've forgotten someone's name right after being introduced.

While good note taking ensures that information sticks around for future retrieval, even that isn't enough when you're cramming lots of learning into a short time frame. It can be really frustrating. You're trying to get yourself up to speed quickly, but the fact remains that you'll never get proficient if your overwhelmed brain has to remember everything.

That's why I love cheat sheets. These short, one- to two-page documents become reference guides for crucial information you need to rapidly absorb.

The Buyer's Matrix you're developing is a cheat sheet that's focused entirely on your primary decision makers. You can create cheat sheets for a whole host of other topics, including product/service highlights, competitive highlights, as well as specific technologies or processes.

I created the cheat sheet on page 84 for learning about new products. Notice how it includes many of the areas we've already talked about.

A cheat sheet also helps you stay focused while you're learning new information. It reminds you of key facts that you don't want to forget. It's also useful to have handy when you're talking to your prospects for the first time—you're not relying on your own unreliable memory to retrieve and record all of the crucial information you're seeking or delivering in a short span of time.

Furthermore, the very act of creating a cheat sheet helps you internalize information much more quickly. Doing this may make you feel like you're back in high school, but your retention skyrockets when you make this extra effort. Entering the information onto the cheat sheet cements it in your memory.

This practice utilizes several of the learning techniques we covered in chapter 10. The sections on the sheet correspond to the file folders in your brain that categorize this new information, which helps with recall. Writing a cheat sheet also helps you dump the information you've learned in one easily retrievable spot. By doing so, you free yourself up to handle all the additional complexities of your new position.

To make this cheat sheet "stick," review it periodically. At first, you'll want to go through it several times per day to ensure that you remember it. To really make this information come alive for you, combine it with a story. The more places your brain files things, the easier it'll be for you.

Got it? Okay. Next we're going to focus on trigger events, an

CHEAT SHEET

Product/Service: _____

Target Market: _____

Trigger Events: _____

Primary Decision Makers:

_____

_____

	Status Quo 1	Status Quo 2	Status Quo 3
Possible Issues and Challenges			
Business Case for Change			

Important Features/Capabilities

Competitor 1	Competitor 2	Competitor 3

overlooked but invaluable strategy to get business quickly. Pay attention.

> Create cheat sheets to help new info stick in your brain better.

BONUS: Check out my numerous free cheat sheets at www.agile sellingbook.com.

22

TAP INTO THE TRIGGERS

Would you be interested in learning about something that could quickly establish your credibility, shorten your sales cycle, and virtually eliminate competitors? I hope so, because that's just what trigger events can do.

Trigger events fall under the umbrella of "need to know" now information. But they're worthless unless you first understand your buyers and the value of your offering. That's why we had to wait to talk about them.

Trigger events are occurrences that shift an organization's priorities and loosen the grip of the status quo. When they occur, new priorities emerge overnight.

Some trigger events are internal to an organization, such as new executives, bad third-quarter earnings, reorganizations, mergers, product launches, or expansions. Others are external happenings such as legislative changes, new competitors, economic conditions, increased costs of borrowing money, or new technologies.

Trigger events are change catalysts. For example, when a

company decides to relocate, it needs new furniture, cabling, phone systems, printing, and much more. When escalating oil prices wreak havoc with the budget, senior executives issue edicts telling the entire organization to cut costs. Suddenly, everyone is scrambling to reduce expenditures or increase productivity. And, when people get promoted, they want to make a big impact in a short time. That's why they're open to new ideas and new vendors who can help them reach their new goals.

If overcoming the status quo is your biggest challenge, then trigger events are your trump card. By identifying and tracking factors that catalyze change with your ideal prospects, you'll be able to focus your prospecting initiatives on opportunities where you'll have a higher likelihood of success.

How can you determine what trigger events are important for you and what you're selling? To get started, ask yourself these questions or brainstorm them with colleagues:

1. What goals, objectives, or initiatives do our best customers have in common? Perhaps they're focused on business drivers such as entering new markets, growing sales or market share, or improving operational efficiency. If that's the case, you'll want to pay attention to those newsworthy triggers.

2. What challenges did our best customers face before they changed? Were they struggling with declining profits, increased competition, or changing marketplace demographics? Maybe inefficient processes or changing customer requirements were causing problems? These related issues are also triggers you should be on the alert for.

3. If we look at our fast-moving sales, were there any com-

mon precipitating events? You want to find out what created the urgency. Why, after doing nothing for so long,
did these organizations suddenly decide they had to take
action? Look for and monitor the catalyst behind the
change.

Another way to stimulate thinking about trigger events is to
review local business journals or trade magazines. As you're going through such publications, ask these questions:

- What's the trigger event that's in this article?
- What might this company need to change because of
  what's happening?
- Could it possibly create a need for our offering?

Personally, I discovered that the following trigger events created new business opportunities for me: company growth, stag-
nant sales, product launches, and new sales VPs. Knowing this,
I stopped prospecting promiscuously and focused my efforts on
companies that were experiencing these trigger events.

Here's the good news. Many triggers are public knowledge;
you can read about them on company or business news Web
sites. Because of this, you can use a variety of online alert services (for example, Google Alerts, InsideView, or DiscoverOrg)
to notify you immediately when they occur. For example, I have
an ongoing alert for "new VPs of sales" in "technology companies" because they create new opportunities for me.

Remember, trigger events are catalysts. Companies may not
yet be ready to buy, but they certainly are experiencing changes
that could create an opportunity for you to sell them something.

By getting in the door early, you have a chance to turn a trigger event into a sale.

> Trigger events loosen the grip of the status quo and catalyze change.

BONUS: Download my free *Hidden Gems* e-book to learn more about trigger events: www.agilesellingbook.com.

23

FIND THE FORUMS

Sometimes it's difficult to interview customers directly. Maybe they're too busy. Perhaps their information is confidential and can't be shared. If that's the case, don't worry. You're not out of luck. There are many ways you can still learn from customers unobtrusively, including this next strategy for gathering "need to know" information.

Check out the many online professional forums (such as LinkedIn and professional association sites) where your buyers are discussing issues and challenges, sharing resources, and commiserating with one another about business. The information and stories you can learn there in a short period of time are invaluable.

Ask your colleagues if they know any specific forums targeted to your industry (for example, software, medical) or to the specific positions (CFOs, safety directors) you sell to. Alternatively, you can do your own online search to find them.

When you start spending time in the forums, be an observer. Check out the discussions to find out which topics and issues are hot. Dig into customers' uncensored perspectives, concerns, and questions. It's not often that you get access to this free-flowing information. Many times, because you're in sales, people won't tell you this stuff because they're afraid you'll pounce on them and start pitching. But in the forums, there's security and, often, anonymity.

You can also mine the historical data in the forum by searching for the key words and topics that are relevant to your product and service. Find out what's been said in the recent past too. This can help you seriously condense your learning time.

Once you have a good sense of how these forums run and what participants discuss, you can jump in more actively. Don't be afraid to ask questions. Your fellow forum members could provide valuable insights into questions like these:

- What's your number-one priority this quarter?
- How do you decide when it's time to change or upgrade?
- What are the most important criteria to consider when making decisions on [insert product/service]?
- What kinds of things are you doing to improve efficiency in your operations?
- What are the primary factors making it difficult for you to achieve your goals?

If you post a question, make sure you stay involved in the discussion. Thank people for their insights. Ask for additional clarification. Add your own thoughts and opinions to ongoing discussions too. This encourages people to share and it's good behavior for forum participants.

While these forum members may never be your actual prospects, they are invaluable sources of information that you can't get anywhere else. The more you listen to what's being said, the greater depth of knowledge you'll have about what really matters. After a short period of time, you'll have rich insights into their issues, challenges, goals, and aspirations—key information that can be leveraged to initiate more (and better) conversations.

> Forums provide deep insights
> into potential buyers.

24

CEMENT YOUR KNOWLEDGE

A t this point, you may be impressed by how much information you've collected—and overwhelmed in wondering how
you're going to remember it all. It's important to keep
checking in on your ability to remember all of this information.
As we've seen, your brain has serious limitations on how much
information it can hold at a time. That's why I recommend using
multiple strategies to assimilate new knowledge quickly. It's the
best way to ensure that you can recall and leverage this new info
at a later date.

Here's one approach that works really well: When you're
deep in study mode, stop every thirty minutes to review what
you've just learned. Repeat the information you just covered out
loud to yourself. This helps cement it in your brain even more
when you want to recall it.

Let's say you just read about trends affecting your customer
base and took a few notes. You could quickly move on to the next
topic. But if you want to remember what you read later, take time
now to talk about it. Describe what you just read. If there was a

story about a company that's being negatively impacted by these trends, repeat the story to yourself. If another firm is capitalizing on these trends already, explain what they're doing and why.

The more visual and verbal pictures you can create, the better. Your brain lights up with these vivid descriptions and then files them away in multiple storage places for future retrieval. Now, when you need to remember this info, it's not just stored in an obscure corner of your memory bank.

Another strategy that will help you retain information better is to connect what you're learning to what you already know. As you're studying all this new information, keep asking yourself questions like these:

- What does this remind me of?
- How is it similar to something else I've sold before?
- In what ways is this decision maker similar to other people I've worked with?
- Who does this buyer type make me think of?

As I'm writing this, these questions remind me of a company I worked with a few years back. They were introducing new, groundbreaking technology that was vastly different from what they'd been selling to that point. Most of the long-term sales pros were really struggling—except Jim. He was on fire!

When I asked Jim about his success in a seemingly difficult field, he told me that initially, selling the new product had been hard. Then he recalled a time, more than thirty years earlier, when he had been in the same situation, selling an unfamiliar product. Jim reflected on the strategies he'd used back then to dominate his market and realized that with some slight adjustments, they could work for him again in his new role.

Bingo. Instead of assuming all that new technology was impossible to learn, Jim had a workable filing system he was able to reuse to get up to speed quickly with the new technology. This strategy helped him dominate selling a new product.

Don't keep rushing blindly forward, trying to cram even more facts and figures into your already overflowing head. Stop at regular intervals and use connect-the-dot strategies to cement new learning and reaccess old knowledge.

> Connect what you're learning with
> what you already know.

25

TAKE THE GOBBLEDYGOOK TEST

ere comes the true test of what you've learned so far. Up until now, we've focused on "need to know" now info along with strategies to make remembering easier. To be a successful seller, though, you can't just ingest the information. It's what you do with it that counts. If your knowledge is stuck inside you, it's worthless. If it comes out as a bunch of mumbo jumbo, you blow it too.

When I first started in technology sales, it was all gobbledygook to me. I couldn't even remember the difference between hardware and software. But, after going through my training class and spending time studying the lingo, systems, and product attributes, I thought I was ready for prime time. I was wrong. When I tried to explain things to prospects, I'd get totally bogged down in irrelevant details. When I tried to answer their questions, I would discover serious knowledge gaps. Sometimes what I said didn't even make sense to me!

Until you can clearly articulate things so that both you and your prospects can understand them, you're going to struggle. There's only one way to prevent that from happening: Every time you learn something new, test yourself by trying to explain it to someone else. Not only does this make the learning stick (which we've already talked about), but it also forces you to process the information in your own words. Don't move on until you can explain things clearly, without stumbling over your own explanations.

Now, let's take this a step further. Below are four questions that your prospects will inevitably ask you about your products or services. If you don't prepare for them up front, you're virtually guaranteed to sound like a total mush-mouth. That doesn't inspire a lot of confidence. However, if you can answer these correctly, efficiently, and with confidence, you're demonstrating that you've achieved situational credibility.

- **What does your company do?**
  Your challenge: In three minutes, tell your prospect what you do from their perspective. They don't want to know that you sell software or accounting services. They want to know what kinds of companies you work with and how you help them.
- **What are your primary products/services?**
  Your challenge: In three minutes, give your prospects an overview of one of your offerings. What is it? What does it do? How does it work? Your job is to make it so understandable that a novice would get it. (Note: If you have multiple products/services, repeat this for each one.)

- **Why should I consider changing from my current way of doing things?**

  Your challenge: In three minutes, share the challenges and issues that your targeted prospects typically encounter with their status quo. Then expand on that by talking about the outcomes people get from using your products/services.

- **Have you worked with other companies like ours before?**

  Your challenge: In three minutes, tell a short customer success story. Make sure the prospects know how the customer handled things before you worked with them, the issues they had, and the value they're getting now.

Fighting gobbledygook is a never-ending battle. Every time you learn something new, you need to figure out how to articulate it to others. Make sure you're speaking in plain English. It's so easy to slip in acronyms or industry-specific terminology that normal people don't understand.

Recently, I spoke at a sales kickoff meeting for a company that sold to eye doctors. Before my session, two of their customers talked to the sales force. I'll never forget the doc who said, "You speak sales rep talk, full of all these scientific terms I don't understand. It either makes me feel stupid or I don't care about it. I speak doctor talk. That's my language. And I have to convert everything to patient talk."

In short, he was imploring these salespeople to drop the technical terms and marketing-speak. It was all gobbledygook to him. He wanted straight talk, something he could easily understand tied to what mattered most to him.

One more thing. Not only do you have to figure out the most important points, but you also have to figure out what to leave out. Otherwise, you babble on and on, boring people to death. At the same time, you need to make sure you're not oversimplifying.

That's why it's so important to make sure that what you know is understandable to others. If we don't do our own gobbledygook tests, we'll flunk in front of our best prospects.

> Tell others what you're learning before you tell your prospects.

26

RECOGNIZE THE "ENOUGH" POINT

How do you know when your deep dive is done? At the beginning of this section, we talked about its being a thirty-day process. However, it really depends on the complexity of your product or service offerings and how new you are to a particular field. Occasionally it can take days; more often, your learning extends for months. No matter the case, though, you can't wait until you know everything before you actually get out there and start selling.

Remember, the goal is to get you to the point of situational credibility, where you can have a decent conversation with a prospect or customer. From a learning perspective, your first two to four weeks will be the most brutal. But in this time, you'll develop the key learning skills and techniques to keep your information-gathering skills nimble.

So when have you reached the "enough" point? You're ready to start focusing on activities that bring in revenue when you're able to:

- Give an overview of your products or services.
- Describe your prospect's typical status quo, including its strengths and weaknesses.
- Identify those involved in the decision process, as well as their goals, issues, and challenges.
- Clearly express the value your customers get from using your offering.
- Share several stories of real customers who are benefiting from working with you.
- Identify trigger events that change your prospect's priorities.

You need to be able to articulate this information out loud. Just because you know something doesn't necessarily mean you can explain it well. It's only when you can speak confidently and accurately about these main points that you've learned "enough" to actually start selling.

Also, please realize that you'll never feel perfectly ready for prime time. No one ever does. It's literally impossible to cram everything into your head in a short time. Your prospects don't expect perfection. They just want to work with someone who can answer their questions, bring them expertise, and take care of them. Rather than beating yourself up for your inability to remember it all, use those cheat sheets you created. Become a master of knowing where and how to find things. If you can deliver that, you're good to go.

So far, we've been concentrating almost exclusively on knowledge acquisition. You may not realize it yet, but the strategies you've put into action over the last thirty days have set the foundation for your sales success. You're a more agile learner and already a better seller, because you've focused on what matters most—to both you and your customers.

In essence, you've learned how to learn quickly. When marketplace directions or economic conditions change, you'll be ready to quickly adapt. When new products or services are introduced, you'll be one of the first to figure out how to sell them. When you change jobs, you'll know how to take the deep dive so you can quickly get up to speed. While the rapid learning process may seem ponderous at first, it's much easier next time.

Now, we're going to switch gears and focus on selling skills. What's needed after your deep dive is actual customer engagement. At this point, you should be talking to prospects, sharing what you know, and finding out what you don't. These dialogues cement this new information in your brain, and point out what else you need to learn.

As we've already talked about, buyers are pretty picky these days. You can't just start blathering about everything you've learned. Instead, you need to leverage your knowledge so you can have intelligent conversations with your prospects.

If you're new to selling, this can be challenging. Please realize, it's also very doable. For those who have been selling for a while, listen up. Your buyers' expectations have changed and unless you do too, you may find yourself in deeper trouble than you thought possible at this point in your career.

So now that you've hit the "enough" point, let's turn our focus on to sales skills.

> You'll never know "enough," but
> don't let that stop you.

Part 4

Pick Up New Skills Fast

Getting better faster matters. Agile sellers swiftly ferret out what works, and at the same time they focus on continuous improvement. The goal? Maximum impact with each buyer interaction.

27

SPEAKING ABOUT SALES

Every seller is chartered with bringing revenue into the company. That's what you're paid for. You're not compensated for building relationships, solving your customers' problems, or helping them achieve their objectives. Yet these activities determine if you're successful or not—and you can't do them well unless you truly understand how your offering impacts your customer. That's why the thirty-day learning immersion is so necessary. Now that you have those skills down, we'll build from there.

This section focuses on getting better at sales quickly. It's written very differently from the previous section because learning a new skill is different from acquiring knowledge. Selling is actually a complex set of skills. To be successful, a seller has to leverage new info appropriately, add value, lead discussions, reduce risk, differentiate from competitors, and much more. What you do changes based on whom you're talking to, what's important to them, their responses, and a host of other factors. And you have to do all this in real time, because your income depends on it.

In sales, the key to long-term success is short-term success. Getting better faster really matters in this profession.

Each of the next seventeen chapters features a different rapid learning strategy designed to speed up your path to proficiency. In many cases, I've shared real-life examples, because, as I said earlier, stories help your brain remember things better. Further, they offer proof that these tools really do work.

Regardless of how long you've been selling, you'll find strategies that you can use:

- If you're a seasoned pro, you'll discover shortcuts to help you sell new products or services in record time.
- If you've struggled with sales before, you'll get good ideas for increasing your success rate.
- If you're just starting out, you'll find a multitude of ways to help you meet and exceed your quota.

Some of the early strategies presented are foundational; make sure to check them out before moving on. The rest are meant to pick and choose from. Some will resonate better with you; they'll align with how you like to learn. Others will be more applicable to your current situation. All of them accelerate your sales success.

If your company has a quality onboarding program that includes sales training, you're lucky. Even if you do, however, what you find in the following chapters will help expedite your learning process. If you're like most people, though, you're pretty much left on your own to figure it out in your new role. That's why so many sellers struggle. Left to their own devices, they do what they think salespeople should do: make calls and pitch products. They may even hate doing it, but that's what they

658.85 KONKATA

Come join us in the Teen room for snacks, crafts and fun

Family Night: Games and Goodies
Tuesday, January 27th, 6:00 pm - 8:30 pm or 9:
Come join us in the Children's and Teen Rooms on Tues
night of board games, cards, snacks and hot cocoa! We w
bring some of your own. All ages are invited.

CHILDREN'S PROGRAMS

***ALL CHILDREN'S PROGRAMS REQUIRE PR
may sign up your children either in person or by phor

Monday Night Children's Chess Club
Mondays, January 12th and 26th, 6:00 pm - 8:00 pm
Winter Chess Tournament Monday, January 5th, 5:
Learn chess from a master! From learning the movement
program will give beginners and experienced players age
the game. Senior chess master Mikhail Perelsteyn will be

think it takes. They're wrong, but they don't know better. Then, when it doesn't work, they decide they're just not cut out to sell and quit.

That's sad, because it doesn't have to end that way. Virtually anyone can learn how to sell with the right information, motivation, and guidance. What you'll find here are the strategies that'll keep you headed in the right direction and enable you to find sales success much faster. That's what being an agile seller is all about.

> The key to long-term success
> is short-term success.

28

FIND YOUR STARTING POINT

A s a skill, sales is too complex to focus on in its entirety. That's why the most important thing you can do at the front end is to chunk it down and then sequence your learning.

Earlier, in chapter 20, we explored the buyer's journey and the four primary decisions they made. As you'll see below, each one of these primary decisions has a corresponding stage in the sales process.

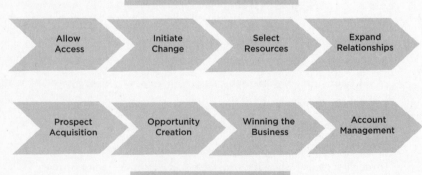

BUYER'S DECISIONS

| Allow Access | Initiate Change | Select Resources | Expand Relationships |

| Prospect Acquisition | Opportunity Creation | Winning the Business | Account Management |

SALES PROCESS

Each stage or chunk of the sales process has a very different objective. This means that you need to leverage very different skill sets as you progress through your customer's buying journey.

1. Prospect Acquisition: At this stage, your objective is to initiate a conversation with someone who has the potential to be a good customer. To do that, you need to move your prospect from oblivious to curious. Your company may start the process with online lead generation or it may begin with your own outreach efforts. Sales skills for this stage include networking, prospecting, targeting, and researching.

2. Opportunity Creation: At this stage, your job is to aid prospects in determining if making a change is worthwhile for their company. To do so, you need to move them from complacency to deciding that the status quo needs to go. Key sales skills include questioning, business case development, getting buy-in, and creating value.

3. Winning the Business: Your role here is to help prospects understand why working with you and your company is the best choice. This step requires you to guide prospects from considering a wide variety of options to feeling certain that you're the right resource. Key sales skills include presenting, differentiating, negotiating, addressing obstacles, and competitive strategy.

4. Account Management: Your objective in this stage is to expand your account presence. This means you need to first ensure your customer's satisfaction and then locate additional sales opportunities within the company. Key skills include customer service, proactive problem solving, and opportunity identification.

You can't become a good seller by focusing on all these skills concurrently. Your challenge is to identify the one area you can tackle right now that will make a quantifiable difference in your success. Consider these factors in making your choice.

First Things First. If you have to develop your own client base, your immediate emphasis should be on prospect acquisition skills. Your focus should be on getting better at setting up meetings. Until you're talking to an actual prospect, everything else is a moot point.

Sometimes the job you're in dictates what stage you start with. If you're following up on leads generated by another person, you need to determine where the prospects are in the buyer's journey. If they're considering a change, focus first on opportunity creation skills. If the prospect is further along in the journey and seriously looking at options, focus on skills that help you win the business. If you're hired for account management, work on those skills first.

Set the Sequence. Follow the buying journey. If you prospected successfully, you'll soon be having conversations with potential clients. You must assume that at most, they're only interested in learning whether a change could help their organization. That means your next focus should be on opportunity creation skills. Once prospects decide a change is worthwhile, then turn to those skills that look more specifically to winning the business.

Fix Problem Areas. No matter how long you've been in sales, there's always room for improvement. Ask yourself these questions to determine the best sales skills to focus on initially:

• Are you satisfied with your prospecting results? If not, you need to figure out what's causing your problems and how you can change.

- Are enough of your initial conversations turning into serious discussions? If there's a big drop-off, consider what you can do to get better results.
- Do you lose to "no decision" frequently? If too many forecasted prospects decide to stay with their status quo, focus on opportunity creation skills.
- Are competitors beating you up? If so, look at improving those sales skills that help you win the business.
- Are your existing customers growing? If not, it's time to get to the root cause of why you're not expanding the services you offer to those customers and brainstorm ways you can change that.

Now, let's dig into those rapid learning strategies that'll help you master selling a whole lot faster.

> Identify one area to improve
> that will make a quantifiable difference.

29

FOCUS ON PERSONAL BESTS

Sales is a numbers game, or so the popular saying goes. If you just make enough calls, have enough meetings, and give enough presentations, you'll succeed. Best of all, every no you hear brings you that much closer to a yes.

If only things were that simple. Unfortunately, sheer quantity isn't the best indicator of future success. When I was at Xerox, I found it fascinating that top performers actually made fewer calls and had fewer prospects than their average counterparts. How could that be? It defied the very maxims I was hearing about sales success.

It took a while to figure out that these top sellers simply focused on targeting better prospects and maximizing each conversation. Their examples started me thinking about creating more meaningful sales metrics—personal bests, or PBs.

The first time I heard about PBs was when my then eight-year-old daughter joined the local swim team. As a neophyte, her backstroke and freestyle left a lot to be desired. But she didn't fret about losing races because her coach kept her attention on PBs. Each week, her goal was to drop time in her races—not win, but beat her own personal best. Sometimes she only cut one-tenth of a second from her previous performance, but it was an improvement nonetheless and worth celebrating.

I loved this viewpoint and so did she. Because I'm sales obsessed, I immediately saw its application for salespeople. Instead of just focusing on quantity, we'd be much better off if we emphasized improvement metrics where we could continually strive for personal bests.

For example, you could work on achieving PBs in the following areas:

- Connection Ratio: What percentage of calls/contacts turn into initial conversations? The more calls you can convert to conversations, the fewer calls you'll need to make.
- Initial Meeting Conversion: What percentage of your initial meetings have an immediate follow-up scheduled? The higher this number, the fewer prospects you'll need.
- Length of Sales Cycle: How long does it take to close a deal? The longer deals are in your pipeline, the less likely prospects are to do business with you.
- Closing Ratio: How many of your initial meetings actually turn into customers? If you can close a higher percentage of sales, you'll be much more successful.
- Losses to No Decision: What percentage of your forecasted prospects stay with the status quo? Lowering this ratio brings in more revenue.

What's notable about these kinds of goals is that you can sequence them, which is an important factor in rapid learning. For example, in a new sales job, you'd clearly want to start out with your Connection Ratio. If you turn more of your calls into conversations, you'll be assured of a steady stream of new prospects. Don't just measure how many calls you're making or e-mails you're sending. Go deeper. Ask "What percentage are currently converting?" Once you have a baseline, the logical next question becomes "How can I get more to convert into initial conversations?"

With this on your mind, become a student of prospecting. Deconstruct your messages into their component parts: introduction, body, and close. Identify factors that could affect your success, such as subject line, length, tone, appearance, and grammar. Every one of these elements could impact your Connection Ratio. What can you do to get a PB? How can you get better results from the same number of or fewer contacts?

Once you've asked yourself these crucial questions, immerse yourself in prospecting. Read articles about it. Talk to colleagues about what's working for them. Listen in on different people's approaches. Ask for feedback on what you could improve. Then start experimenting. Change things up. And, especially, pay attention to what gets better responses. Your goal is to set a PB next week or next month—and that won't happen if your only focus is on the sheer number of calls you're making.

Once you're satisfied with your Connection Ratio, move on to improving your Initial Meeting hit rate. From a sequencing perspective, it's the logical next step. One thing at a time.

By constantly maintaining a PB mind-set, your time to proficiency for a particular sales skill will get shorter and shorter.

Before you know it, you'll be really good in that one element of selling and be able to apply that agility and momentum to other parts of your sales process.

> Use personal bests as a way to
> track your improvement.

30

PREP WITH PASSION

There are few things in life that make me want to get up on a soapbox, but the importance of preparation is one of them. Planning matters. Top sellers invest significantly more time prepping for meetings than their less successful counterparts. That's why they get the results they do. They've committed to achieving the best possible results in every client interaction.

Prospects can quickly determine if you've done your homework. They're constantly assessing whether your conversation is aligned with their objectives and priorities. They're also evaluating you personally: Are you adding value, offering insights, sharing relevant information, and simplifying the complex? Are you making good use of your time together? Remember, *you* are the differentiator today, not your product or service.

Prior to any meeting, research is crucial. Check out the company's Web site to get insights into its business direction, trends, and challenges. Research the individuals you'll meet to learn as much as you can about them. If your company has a marketing automation system, review your prospect's prior interactions

MEETING PLAN

Outcome:

You: At the end of this meeting, the next step will be:_____

_____

Prospect: They're expecting:_____

Opening: Make intros, confirm times, review agenda.

Set the Stage: Share your value proposition, success stories, ideas, or insights. Your goal is to establish yourself as a credible resource. Write down what you'll say.

Transition: How will you transition to questions?

Focus on Business: Lead a conversation about the reason for meeting. List ten questions you want to discuss in a logical sequence.

Identify needed support materials such as presentations, handouts, case studies.

Determine who needs to be there (your/their company).

Advance the Process: Bring the meeting to a close on a timely basis. Summarize your understanding, open issues, etc. Suggest the logical next step.

with your content. Figure out what you can about where they are in their decision process: Are they simply curious, considering a change, or seriously looking at options? If you're talking to an existing customer, find out if they've had any recent service or billing problems.

Research provides context. You can get a good sense of who your prospects are and what's important to them. Preparation, however, also involves leveraging this context to determine the best possible approach for your prospect. As you prepare for the meeting, ask yourself these questions:

- Where's this prospect now?
- Where are their likely desired outcomes?
- What will it take to get them there?
- What are their expectations?

Next, get clear on *your* desired outcome of the meeting. From your perspective, what's the logical next step? By making an educated, research-based assessment of where the prospect is in their buying journey, you'll know what to shoot for in the meeting. Perhaps it's an in-depth analysis, a follow-up meeting with additional personnel, or a product demonstration. Knowing your objective helps you plan your upcoming conversation.

Finally, in preparing, map out how you'd like to see the actual meeting run, taking into consideration the time frame you have to work with. A planning sheet I developed to help me get ready for initial meetings appears on page 117. You can easily modify it for any type of conversation.

It's a lot of work to map out a meeting in such detail, but it yields results. Time invested here has high payback, and regardless of the stage you're at in your career, it's a good practice to maintain. I've seen sellers go into meetings thinking that they don't need to do their homework; their charismatic personality will carry the day. It doesn't. That strategy helps you achieve mediocrity, at best. I don't recommend it!

Mapping out meetings is useful even though meetings rarely turn out exactly as you planned. Planning enables sales agility. It provides a foundation for your meeting at the same time as it gives you the flexibility to move in a new direction. With an actual plan in place, you're free to follow new directions when they arise, and can quickly recalibrate and get the conversation back on course when it strays.

> The quality of your planning determines the outcome you achieve.

31

CONNECT WITH QUESTIONS

Questions are the capstone of sales agility. Throughout this book, I use numerous questions to stretch your thinking. By actively engaging with them, you learn more and faster. I've also shared some very specific questions designed to deepen your knowledge base and give you a rock-solid sales foundation.

Questions are also crucial in the sales process itself. But traditional questions like "Tell me about your company" or "What keeps you up at night?" are no longer effective. Today's buyers look down on you if they have to provide information that's readily available online. Buyers also hate smarmy questions like "If I can show you a way to save 25 percent, would you buy from me?" It signals that you have nothing to offer.

On the other hand, if you ask your prospects insightful and thought-provoking questions, you'll get a totally different reaction. Your credibility will soar. You'll be seen as a caring person who has their best interests at heart. The prospect will consider you an asset who's capable of providing value beyond that of your product or service.

The ability to ask powerful questions is a "need to know" now skill. It has an immediate and positive impact on the entire sales process. Unfortunately, you can't expect good questions to magically pop out of your mouth when you're in the midst of an important conversation. Your brain is incapable of both listening intently and formulating what to ask next. It does one or the other.

Because the quality of your questions ultimately determines the quality of your conversation, it's imperative to plan them ahead of time. Certainly the questions you choose to ask will be dependent on what you're selling and where your prospects are in their buying process. There are, however, some key factors to consider in planning your questions, regardless of what you're selling.

Focus: From your prospect's perspective, good conversations are all about them. They explore, evaluate, and pinpoint what matters most to their company and the individuals involved in making any change. Here's what you need to be asking about:

- Status quo relevant to your offering
- Issues and aspirations you can impact
- Business value of making a change
- Possible solutions, ideas they've considered
- Perceptions of priorities, risk, vendors
- Where they are in their buying journey

Asking these questions enables you to shape and refine your approach as you move forward. Yes, it's all about being agile and relentlessly relevant.

Context: Use your knowledge and research to set up your questions. This positions you as a much more valuable asset. Here are two examples:

- "In researching your account, I noticed that shrinking time to market is a key objective this year. What impact is this having on your area?"
- "Last week you downloaded our white paper, *Improving Sales Conversion Rates*. What's driving your interest in that topic right now?"

Sequence: As you plan your questions, pay attention to the order in which you ask them. To get the conversation rolling, start out with easy questions such as, "What are the biggest challenges your salespeople are having with prospecting?" Your next question should always be a logical extension of the previous one; it's what keeps the conversation flowing. For example, a good follow-up to the previous question would be, "What have you done so far to help them improve their prospecting skills?"

Before your meeting, review all your questions. Think about how you'd answer them if you were the prospect. Would they get you talking? About what? Do they make you think? Do they feel manipulative? After your conversation, analyze what worked and what didn't. If a question yielded a "stupid" answer, change it. If it didn't elicit the information you'd hoped for, try phrasing the question a different way or plan follow-up questions.

Proficiency at asking crucial questions allows you to be even more agile throughout the sales cycle. It's well worth the effort, don't you think?

> Insightful questions build credibility
> and deepen relationships.

32

PRACTICE SAFE SELLING

Selling is a soft skill. Because sales involves people, it's about effectively communicating, influencing, strategizing, getting buy-in, and so much more. And, because everyone has different life experiences, goals, personalities, work environments, and expectations, it's tough to figure out the best approach to use at any given time.

In *The Little Book of Talent,* Daniel Coyle writes: "Soft skills are built by playing and exploring inside challenging, ever-changing environments. These are places where you encounter difficult obstacles and respond to them over and over, building the network of sensitive wiring you need to read, recognize and react."

I totally agree with him. Getting better at selling requires so much more than just learning the procedures. We need deliberate practice to achieve proficiency. According to skill acquisition research, we need to conduct these simulations in an environment that replicates, as well as possible, what we'll actually face on the job. It's only by practice that we can acquire the sales skills and agility necessary for ongoing success.

Unfortunately, the majority of salespeople won't practice their soft skills because they despise role-playing. They say it's artificial and not like what happens in real life. They'll also tell you how they hate making fools of themselves in front of their colleagues. But if they don't practice, their first run-through of any new approach is in real time with actual prospects. Definitely not the best strategy!

Deliberate role-playing is the only way to get better at selling. It's embarrassing—and costly—to practice in front of prospective clients. Believe me, looking stupid in front of supportive colleagues is a whole lot better than looking stupid in front of prospects.

Recently, I launched a new service that was targeted at VPs of marketing. I was pretty excited about it, especially after quickly landing a meeting with the head marketer of a well-known technology firm. But I soon found out that I wasn't ready for the conversation I needed to have with him.

How did I find that out? I called up a colleague and asked her to role-play with me. Using the Buyer's Matrix, I gave her a quick overview of what was important to this person, and then we began the simulation. Just a few minutes into our conversation, I could tell I was digging my own grave. I was babbling about what the program entailed and how we'd work together. Gobbledygook. When my colleague asked me questions about my offering, I stumbled over my answers, which only seemed to raise more issues and concerns. It wasn't too long after that that she brushed me off, telling me to send her some more information for future reference. Some friend! But it was what I needed—clearly I wasn't ready to have this conversation with the actual prospect.

Doing that role-play was crucial to my ultimate success. It

forced me to rethink and restructure what I wanted to cover in my upcoming meeting. The changes I made led to an entirely different conversation and a much better outcome. Instead of blowing it, I nailed it.

Role-playing helps you hone your skills and increase your effectiveness. You can use it to improve your phone and in-person conversations, demonstrations, negotiations, and more. It's really invaluable to build your soft skills through repetition and trial and error. Enlist your colleagues to play your prospects. Ask them to listen, participate, and react as if they were the person you're meeting.

Role-playing scenarios also allow you to stop if you stumble—and smooth over whatever element you screwed up. Rather than continuing, you can go back to where the problem began and start that section over again. Do it over and over until you get it right. Doing a pause-rewind sequence prevents your brain from allowing bad behavior to become a bad habit.

After the role-playing exercise, ask the person who's playing your customer for feedback. Try asking questions that will specifically point out what worked and didn't work in your conversation, such as:

- Did what I said make sense, or was it confusing?
- Did it interest or engage you? Why or why not?
- If you were to make one suggestion for my presentation, what would it be?
- How could I have elicited a different response?
- What could I do to make it more of a conversation?
- In your opinion, what did I do well?
- Would you have taken the logical next step with me? Why or why not?

Listen to what your colleagues say and note where you can improve what you're doing. Run the role-play until the material is ingrained in your brain and you're comfortable with it.

Role-playing isn't always fun, especially when others are evaluating you. But it's an investment in yourself that truly does make a difference.

> Deliberate practice increases sales effectiveness exponentially.

33

REMOVE THE BLINDERS

Sometimes we're totally oblivious to our own shortcomings. It's not intentional; we just see things our way while our prospects have a whole different perspective. Fortunately, there are some more ways, besides role-playing, that we can reduce the chances of a disconnect between what we say and what our prospects hear.

Take Katie, for example. She worked for a small business services firm and was just moving into a business development position. An important prospect was coming to the office on Monday morning for a big meeting that Katie had been asked to kick off. After her introduction, her coworkers would provide a program overview. Despite having only ten minutes on the agenda, her role was crucial. She needed to set the right tone as well as convey that her firm had a good grasp of the client's challenges.

On Sunday night, Katie went to the office to run through her brief presentation in the exact room where they'd be meeting. She wanted to simulate the actual event as accurately as possible, knowing it would increase her confidence. After going through it a few times, she decided to record herself opening the meeting.

When Katie watched the recording, she was appalled. Instead of coming off like a real pro as she'd imagined, her discomfort with the content was obvious. She'd forgotten to include several key points. She used lots of "um" and "uh" fillers. Her transitions to the next slides were sloppy.

In short, she had no idea how the prospect would see her until she took a serious look at herself. By removing her blinders, she uncovered multiple areas for improvement.

Katie kept practicing into the night, and then recorded herself again. Her presentation was better, but still lacked the professionalism she'd hoped to convey. She continued running through the kickoff, again and again, each time reviewing the video to spot where she needed to smooth out her presentation. She didn't quit until she knew she was ready for prime time.

The next day, Katie aced the kickoff.

As sellers, we often race from call to call or meeting to meeting, getting ready just in the nick of time. Our failure to stop and review what we're doing from our prospect's perspective can actually hurt our ability to be successful.

I'll never forget the first time I saw myself on video. It was painful to watch. During the role-play, I twirled my hair around my fingers numerous times. I kept taking my ring off and putting it back on. Instead of coming off as calm, cool, and collected, I saw my nervous habits betray my true feelings. So I tied my hair back, removed my ring, and tried again.

Getting rid of those distractions helped, but also revealed another major problem. Viewing the role-play from my prospect's perspective, my presentation felt like an inquisition, not a conversation. Ugh! If I were the prospect, I wouldn't want to talk with me again. Fortunately, I had time to make changes before I went to my meeting.

To get up to speed quickly, we need multiple forms of deliberate practice. Role-plays are essential. Filming your role-play provides an even deeper level of feedback. Hearing your own audio is also very helpful, because so much of selling is done over the phone.

But the real judge of our behaviors is our prospect. That's why it's crucial that we review everything we do from their perspective. Are we enticing and engaging? Do we seem credible? Are we adding value? Does our flow make sense? Do we run on and on? Are we understandable? Do we come across as a pro or sound like a cheesy salesperson?

Everyone has the capacity to look at what they're doing from another person's perspective, yet few people take the time. It's simply a matter of making this aspect of preparation a discipline. Get your prep work done earlier than your actual "performance" time so you have a chance to review and improve it. When you do, you'll see rapid progression in your sales success.

> Review what you're doing from your prospect's perspective.

34

PICK THE UPSTART'S BRAIN

I f I were new in a sales position and could interview only one salesperson in the company, I'd hightail it to an upstart. Upstarts are individuals who typically have been in their job for less than three years. Despite not possessing deep expertise when hired, they were able to, in short order, catapult themselves to the top echelons of salespeople.

More important, it wasn't blind luck that got those rookies to the top. Upstarts throw themselves into mastering sales. They crack the code that everyone struggles with and figure out how to win business with today's prospects. Plus, they're not too far removed from being novices themselves (unlike the seasoned pros) and they acutely remember what it took to get started. Often, they're happy to help a newbie.

Years ago, when I first started selling technology, I found two upstarts who saved my butt. My nontechnical mind was having difficulty assimilating all the new information that was being thrown at me in such a helter-skelter fashion. Despite having a very successful sales career at Xerox, I was stumped about how to prospect using my newfound knowledge. I couldn't even pass my own gobbledygook test. Still, my boss felt otherwise and thought it was time for me to start making calls.

Enter John and Joe. Both had been at the company for a couple years and were doing really well. Clearly, they'd figured out how to successfully prospect in this field. I asked them each for help, and, fortunately, they both agreed to share the secrets to their success. I chose to talk with each one individually, thinking I'd get more ideas that way. I was right. After talking with John and Joe, I had a very clear idea how to get started and before long was setting up lots of meetings.

If you have an opportunity to learn from an upstart, take it. Better yet, seek one out. Before you meet with these very focused, goal-oriented people, prepare your questions. Make sure they are designed to elicit very specific responses on one topic only (for example, prospecting, proposals, or demonstrations). The quality of the information you get with this focus is so much richer. You can always come back later when you're at the next step of the sales process.

When I met with John and Joe, prospecting was my singular focus. I wanted to hear and see what they were actually doing to turn a noninterested person into a prospect. It's been a while since my interview with them, but if I were new in the field today, here's what I'd ask to ensure that I learned exactly what I wanted to:

- How do you identify which companies to contact? Are there any specific criteria you use?
- Who are the primary decision makers you want to meet with? Why? Is one position more important than the others?

- What kind of research do you do prior to initiating contact? What are you looking for?
- What's your typical prospecting process? Do you reach prospects by e-mail, phone, events, social media, or another medium?
- Can you give me specific examples of what you say when you contact people by phone? What makes it so effective?
- Can you show me sample e-mails that you use in prospecting? Why did you choose these words?
- If people aren't interested right away, how do you keep in touch? Can you give me examples?
- How do you know when to quit?
- If you actually do connect with a person, how does your message change? What do you do to engage them in a discussion?

Make sure you take copious notes on what the upstarts say and, if possible, get copies of any written messages. You want to be able to replicate them in your own prospecting efforts.

When you're new in a job, the upstarts can be one of your best resources. By picking their brains, you significantly shorten your own learning curve.

> Leverage the upstart's expertise
> to find out what's working.

35

OBSERVE TOP SELLERS

Learning from seasoned pros is a whole lot different from picking the upstart's brain. On the positive side, they have deep, rich expertise collected through years of experience. They also have a longer-term perspective, enabling them to sail much more smoothly through challenging times. But on the downside, it's highly likely that seasoned sellers are unconsciously competent, meaning it's difficult for them to articulate what works. They just seem to "know" what to do next. Also, because they have so many long-term client relationships, what you see happening on any one call may not be indicative of what it actually takes to be successful.

Jennifer found this out the hard way. Her father, Frank, owned a small manufacturing plant that sold clothing items to big-box retailers. One of their salespeople, Marcus, was having his third banner year in a row, raking in big commissions from his only client. You'd think Frank would be delighted with Marcus's performance. He wasn't. He wanted to keep the money in the family.

One day, Frank sent Jennifer out on a sales call with Marcus.

The next day, he fired Marcus. Apparently, his daughter reported back that she could easily handle the account, based on what she observed in the congenial planning meeting with the client and Marcus. Unfortunately, Jennifer had no idea that the relaxed, positive meeting was the result of Marcus's countless hours of preparation, ideation, and implementation.

When Jennifer took over the account, the client quickly realized that she was a lightweight. Within a year, their orders were a mere fraction of what they'd been when Marcus handled their account.

Why am I telling you this? Because there's so much you can learn by talking to top sellers and by watching them in action. The key is to be a smart questioner and a savvy observer. Don't take what you observe at face value without digging into the full context of what you're seeing.

Start by focusing on the part of the sales process where you really need help. For example, if you're losing to "no decision" too much, listen in on top sellers' conversations or attend meetings where this is the topic of discussion. If you're losing to competitors too often, you'll want to participate in calls or events where the seasoned pro is engaged in a tough competitive battle.

To get the most value from your observations, learn as much as you can about how top sellers think and the choices they're making. That's why it's important to ask them questions before you observe them:

- Where is this prospect in their buying process?
- What have you done previously with them to get to this point?
- Have you encountered any stumbling blocks so far? If so, what were they?

- What is the purpose of this upcoming meeting?
- In your opinion, what's a successful outcome?
- Who will we be talking to? Can you tell me a little about each person?
- How are you starting out the conversation? Why did you make that choice?
- What questions will you be asking? Why are they important?
- Do you anticipate any obstacles? If so, what? How will you handle them?

You can also ask these questions for specific sales observations:

- Prospecting: What are you doing to pique curiosity, establish credibility, and engage them in conversations?
- Initial meetings: What's your strategy for getting a prospect interested in making a change?
- Change justification: How are you helping the client assess if a change makes good business sense?
- Risk: What's your approach for minimizing the risk inherent in change initiatives?
- Differentiation: What will you be doing to differentiate yourself, our offering, and our company from the competitors?

By asking these questions beforehand, you'll understand the context of what you're observing. Then, during the meeting, watch how these strategies play out. You'll learn a whole lot more this way.

Finally, after the observation is over, make sure you take

time to debrief with these seasoned pros. Find out their perceptions of what happened and why they feel that way. Talk about any obstacles or surprises too, as well as why they chose to respond the way they did. The more you learn from their thinking and their actions, the quicker you'll achieve proficiency. After all, if they're still in the business, they must be masters of sales agility.

> Learn from the seasoned pro's thinking
> process and buyer interactions.

36

GET OVER YOURSELF

ometimes it's tough to ask for help. That's why when Anika, the CEO of a Web services company and good friend, called me and asked for help, I listened. She had a meeting scheduled with a hot prospect the next morning. It was a big opportunity, larger than most she'd dealt with so far. She was really nervous about it because, just a few days earlier, she'd lost a big deal she'd hoped to win. She wasn't sure why the prospect had chosen a competitor, but they had.

Anika quickly brought me up-to-date on what had transpired in her first meeting. Then she sent me a very nice multipage proposal so I could give her feedback on it. After reviewing it, I asked Anika why her prospect was looking for new options. She wasn't sure. I questioned whether her recommended service was the best fit. She thought so, but couldn't be positive. I asked how well she knew the decision maker. She said they'd had just that one conversation.

Although Anika was planning to close the deal the next day, she couldn't answer any of these important questions. I immediately knew that she was in danger of blowing the sale because she lacked this critical information. So, to prevent that from happening, we went through the issue areas one by one and discussed, very specifically, what she could do at her next meeting to assure the prospect of her expertise.

I told Anika to ask more in-depth questions about her prospect's problems with his current site, why he wanted change, and the business value he hoped to realize from making the investment. Doing this would strengthen their relationship and give her the information she needed to make the right recommendation. I also suggested that Anika wait until her third conversation to give the prospect her proposal and that she scale things back so he could start out with a smaller initial investment. This would reduce risk and enable her to demonstrate her competence. After that, it would be much easier to close the deal for the rest of the project.

It worked. Anika asked better questions at her next meeting, and learned a lot about what the company actually needed and how she could offer value. Afterward, she rewrote the proposal—using what she had learned in their follow-up conversation—and quickly landed the deal. Of course, if she hadn't asked for help, she could have lost this business for good.

Sound familiar? I bet there have been times when you didn't ask for help when you could have used it. Unfortunately, too many of us equate asking for help with weakness, lack of capability, or ineptness. No one wants to look stupid, especially when we're new on a job. Instead, we want to impress our boss, colleagues, and customers.

The lesson is short but simple: You have to get over yourself. There's no way you could possibly know everything when you're just starting a new position or selling a new product or service.

Asking for help is a sign of strength. It's another way to slash your learning curve. Plus, the suggestions you get will enable you to close more deals sooner. That in itself should be reason enough for you to put your pride aside and request the assistance of others.

Ask for help early enough in your selling process so that there's time to make any necessary changes. Luckily, when she contacted me, Anika had the rest of the day to get ready for her big meeting. But she did waste a whole lot of time putting together a proposal that she never used. If she'd asked for help earlier, she would have been further ahead in the game.

Get over yourself and ask for help so you can get better at selling faster.

> Eat your pride; ask for help
> earlier rather than later.

37

INCREASE YOUR PERCEPTIVITY

Zack used to drive me nuts. Even though he was by far the hardest worker on my sales team, he was struggling to meet his quota consistently. Worse, as his boss, I frequently got calls from his prospects saying, "Tell Zack to back off." Although he'd previously been in sales in New York City, he was having trouble adjusting to the people in Minneapolis. His brusque, to-the-point approach didn't mesh well with our more laid-back communication style.

After going out on sales calls with him, I could see why prospects reacted the way they did. Zack was there to sell; it was clear from the moment he opened his mouth. As soon as he discovered even the slightest bit of unhappiness in the prospect's status quo, he'd lean forward and jump into pitch mode. His prospects would immediately lean back, away from him, and cross their arms. That didn't deter Zack.

To Zack, the logical outcome of the prospect's dissatisfaction was a deal with him—and that's the path he was on. Unfortunately, he totally missed the numerous verbal and nonverbal cues they gave him that said otherwise.

Zack liked to be right in people's faces—literally. His prospects didn't like it and neither did I. As we walked to our sales meetings, I had to keep edging away from him to get some more space. He'd immediately close the gap. Before long, he'd walk me right off the sidewalk and into the street. "Zack," I'd say as I pushed him away, "give me some breathing room."

When I actually told him that his behavior and approach was pushy and off-putting, he was shocked. He was totally oblivious to how people reacted to him and how it affected his performance.

Selling is and always will be about dealing with people. After all, it's people who make decisions, not companies. That's why it's so crucial to be conscious of our impact on them. Everything we do either draws them toward us or moves them further away.

When we notice how people are responding to our presence, we get to have a choice: We can either continue down the same path or do something different to change direction. If you notice any of the following signs, it might mean you're not connecting with people as well as you think you are:

- They raise their eyebrows as if skeptical of what you're saying.
- They're fidgeting or tapping their fingers in boredom or impatience.
- Their heads are moving slightly back and forth.
- They sound hesitant or uncommitted in their responses.

- They won't establish eye contact.
- They're leaning back with crossed arms.

If you notice these negative behaviors, you can stop and re-calibrate your direction. Perhaps you could even say something like, "You seem distracted," or "It looks like you've got some hesitation about changing things here." These honest statements are beneficial for both you and your prospect.

On the other hand, if your prospects are leaning in, listening intently, and making direct eye contact with you, that's a positive sign. If the prospect's head is nodding up and down and he or she is speaking enthusiastically, that's good too. When you see these things, you could say, "It looks like this could be helpful to you," or "You must be facing a similar problem to that of the client I was just telling you about." These reinforcements help you make sure you and your client truly are on the same path.

Most of all, recognizing these nonverbal or subtle verbal cues gives you a much better picture of how prospects really feel about your ideas, products, and services. With increased perceptivity, you can be much more agile, making on-the-spot adjustments that can lead to much better sales outcomes.

> Watch people to learn their subtle
> cues and adjust accordingly.

DEVELOP RECOVERY STRATEGIES

Despite all your best planning, you're going to blow it sometimes in your career. I've been on thousands of sales calls and seen it happen way too many times. And the hungrier you are, the more it happens! Here's how a disaster scenario typically unfolds:

You're talking to a prospect, trying hard to be consultative. You ask about his status quo first, trying to learn more about the context of his sales situation. After your prospect responds, you probe a little deeper: "So have you had any issues or challenges with it?" Your prospect nods his head and says, "Yes. Some."

The minute you hear that, your heart jumps. This company has problems you can solve. Hallelujah! Before you know it, you lean forward, filled with excitement, and say, "Oh. You have problems with that? We can help." And then you start babbling away, sharing every little nuance about your product or service that you think will impress him.

Your prospect immediately senses the change. You're pitching; the conversation is over. He needs to protect himself now.

Within moments, he asks, "How much does it cost?" When you respond, he answers, "Oh. Too bad. It's not in the budget."

I'm sure you know what I'm talking about. You'd think that after all these years I'd be immune to getting stuck in this situation, but I sometimes still get overly excited about an opportunity too. That's a dangerous sign, a key indicator that we're about ready to slip into sales-derailing behavior. When it happens, we need to slam on the verbal brakes or face imminent disaster.

Luckily, I've discovered a recovery strategy that's always gotten me back on track with my prospect. I've taught thousands of sellers to use it the moment they catch themselves droning on about their offering.

"Sorry, Mr. Prospect. Sometimes I just get so excited about how we might be able to help. But I really don't know enough about your business yet. Let's get back to talking about those challenges you mentioned earlier. . . ."

Conclude your recovery statement by asking a specific question related to the issue that started you down this path. Believe it or not, your prospect will probably laugh at your eagerness and accept your apology easily. He'll also appreciate that you nimbly pulled yourself back from the pitch and turned your attention to his business.

When you're new to selling, sometimes it's hard to tell when you're on the path to blowing it. Here are some signs that you could be in trouble:

- You feel a sudden rush of excitement on discovering that your prospect has a "problem."
- You're leaning forward, babbling endlessly about your product/service.

- You're concerned about time and trying to get "everything" in.
- The prospect's arms are crossed and she's leaning back, away from you.
- The prospect's asking all the questions and you're busy explaining things.
- The energy in the room is flat; people are yawning or checking their messages.

Pay attention to when these moments occur in meetings and what you were saying/doing before they happened. Then think: Have you run into the same problem before? Is this a pattern for you?

Recently, I talked with Jeff about an important sales call he had gone on with his tech support guy. Jeff asked his tech guy to explain how they'd handle the migration to the new product. Bad idea. Unbridled tech guys can go on and on, putting every working detail on the table. They can even misjudge polite head nodding as acute interest. Unfortunately, Jeff was unable to recapture his initial momentum and swing the conversation back to the customer's needs. As they left, his prospect said, "Thanks for updating us on what your company is doing. We'll give you a call if we're ever ready to change."

When we went over the sales call later, it became clear that Jeff did not have a recovery strategy in place when his tech guy went off script. To develop one for his next call, I told him he needed three things: 1) better planning, with clearly defined roles for both him and his tech guy; 2) a signal (like a cough or tiny kick) to let his tech guy know to wrap it up; and 3) a phrase Jeff would use to butt in and take control of the conversation.

("Thanks, tech guy, for all the details. Let's get back to talking about the issues you're having with . . .")

It's important to be able to stop ourselves when we're headed into danger. If you don't have a recovery strategy planned, it's harder to get things under control again. Instead, your poor brain flounders, knowing it's in trouble. The stress of the situation prevents it from coming up with ways to change the meeting dynamics.

Believe me, you don't want to be in that position. Develop new approaches for your most common bloopers now and save yourself lots of trouble.

> Develop recovery strategies to deal
> with the inevitable blunders.

39

DARE TO DEBRIEF

was panicking. I'd just spent two hours updating a page on my new Web site and when I saved it, everything was gone. I placed a desperate call to my Web master. When she answered the phone, I frantically rattled off what had transpired. She was quiet for a moment, then slowly said, "Mmm. That's interesting," before lapsing back into silence.

Interesting? The moment she said that, my perspective shifted. I found it interesting that I didn't consider it one bit interesting. Then it hit me how often I see salespeople doing the exact same thing. When they run into sales snafus, they seldom stop to consider what they might have done to create the problem in the first place. They'll look for help. They'll scramble. But they'll rarely say, "Mmm. That's interesting."

Think about what could happen if you were constantly curious about why your prospects reacted the way they did. For example, take that guy you talked to this morning. You were telling him why he should seriously consider changing from his status quo. But he was rude and just "didn't get it."

Mmm. That's interesting. Perhaps he didn't get it because of how you explained the benefits of your service. Maybe you didn't ask enough questions so he felt like you were pushing him to make a decision he wasn't ready to make.

How about those ten new companies you're trying to set up meetings with? You called them last week, then followed up with an e-mail. So far you haven't gotten a response back from anyone.

Mmm. That's interesting. Perhaps a different message would be more effective. Maybe your subject line caused them to delete it. Or could it be that you sounded like a wuss or, worse yet, a product-pushing salesperson? Maybe they're just plain busy and feel that it's your responsibility to get in touch with them.

See where I'm going with this? Whether you're an experienced pro in a new sales position or you're new to selling, you get better faster by continually questioning your results.

As I've said earlier, a common stumbling block you'll face is that your forecasted prospects decide to do nothing. Rock-solid prospects, ones who could really benefit from what you do, choose to stick with their old, not-so-perfect way of doing things. Why would they do that? The reality is, a lot of business is lost because of sloppy selling. To prevent that from happening to you, it's important to regularly debrief after sales meetings.

When you're just getting started, debriefs are more important than ever. Often, you'll have to evaluate your own performance. Sometimes you'll be able to get outside input from a colleague, boss, or trainer who's listening in or at the meeting with you.

Whatever your situation, always be curious about how you could improve your selling ability. Be critical of your own behavior. During your client interactions, pay attention to times when the conversation was challenging for you. Note when things went according to plan or turned out better than you expected. In short, observe your own behaviors while you're doing them. See anything interesting?

To debrief the meeting, try asking yourself or your colleagues these four questions:

1. What did I expect—and what actually happened? If it turned out the way you'd hoped, your planning was likely sufficient. If not, it's a sign you missed something.
2. Where did I run into trouble? Being cognizant of your problem areas is the first step in ensuring you don't make the same mistakes over and over. If you had difficulties in any areas, pay attention.
3. What could I have done differently? Brainstorm some options. Specifically look for ways that you could have improved how you handled things. Better yet, explore ways that you could have eliminated the obstacle entirely.
4. What did I do well? Paying attention to your positive behaviors is important too. You want to be able to repeat them. Also think about how you can enhance what you're already doing well.

Don't just ask these questions when you lose a sale. It's just as important to be curious about what you did to clinch a deal too. Really dig into how you piqued interest, demonstrated value, built the business case, and more. Debrief to find the keys to your success as well.

Staying curious propels you faster on your path to proficiency. It's also what makes you agile and more quickly able to respond to changes as they occur.

> Realize rapid and radical improvement with frequent debriefs.

40

PREVENT EPIC FAILS

So far, we've talked about proactive strategies you can use to ensure that sales conversations go the way you want them to. Many of them involve serious preparation. Plan, test, revise. Plan, test, revise. This is the heart of agility; when you get the fundamentals down pat, you're free to adjust and adapt to changing conditions.

What I haven't mentioned at all is attitude. You've probably heard about the importance of positive thinking. For years, motivational gurus have encouraged us to visualize achieving our goals, making the big sale, beating out competitors. You've got to love that inspirational feeling.

However, thinking positively can backfire on you. Seriously. Recent research by Dr. Gabriele Oettingen, a psychologist at New York University, says that the better you are at visualizing your goals, the less likely you are to achieve them. Visualization can cause your brain to relax; it thinks the hard work has already been done. As a result, you lose focus and clarity, making it much harder to reach your goals.

Instead, Dr. Oettingen discovered that "mental contrasting" works far better than positive thinking alone. Essentially, that means that you're visualizing two things at once:

1. How great it will be to close that big sale (your goal).
2. All the obstacles that stand in the way of achieving that goal.

The incredible power of *negative* thinking is needed to actually prevent epic sales failures, while channeling your good feelings helps you tackle the tasks and activities needed to maximize success.

All the top sellers I know possess a unique balance of positivity and negativity. They're always optimistic about the ultimate outcomes, but they sometimes seem paranoid about everything that could possibly go wrong. That's why they succeed.

To give you a better feel for how they work, try this mental contrasting exercise. Think about an upcoming meeting. First, focus on positive thinking; take a few minutes to visualize yourself walking out of the room or hanging up the phone with a big smile on your face. Your prospects have agreed to move to the logical next step. It's obvious that they want to do business with you.

Next, think about all the obstacles that could prevent you from achieving this outcome. What could possibly go wrong? Write down all your thoughts. You could have technology problems; somebody vocally favors another company; your primary contact was called away at the last minute; six new people show up when you expected one; or your pricing throws them for a loop.

If you've been in sales for a while, you've probably experienced every single one of these obstacles. The first time you faced them, you probably blew the sale. (I'm speaking from experience!) Maybe you've blown it more times than you're willing to admit. Or maybe you've abdicated responsibility for some of them, saying it was beyond your control.

Unfortunately, most people don't take obstacles seriously enough to think through how they could handle them or, better yet, how to prevent them.

For me, technology issues are always showstoppers. If things don't work right the first time, I get discombobulated pretty easily. So now, when I go to meetings, I'm ready to go forward with Plan A, B, or C, depending on what happens. I've learned where my biggest failure points are and ensured they won't happen again.

But that's minor compared with what I think is one of the biggest fails of all—interested people who stay with the status quo. If this is happening to you, it's crucial to ask yourself:

- Why don't they see the value of change?
- How can I build a stronger business case?
- What questions could I ask to help them realize the cost of sticking with the status quo?
- Am I rushing to a solution too quickly?

Challenge yourself to test out different approaches. Remember to envision yourself achieving your goal first. Then get serious about eliminating the obstacles that stand in your way. Your unwavering attention to what could go wrong can actually prevent it from happening.

Use negative thinking to protect against sales-derailing mistakes.

41

MINIMIZE THE MEMORY BURDEN

Feeling a little overwhelmed again? I know the feeling. I used to be a know-it-all. But my memory system failed badly when there became too much to know. Then I became a copious note taker. While that helped, it still wasn't sufficient to keep up with the sheer amount I had to remember.

Cheat sheets came next. They helped me focus on the key points. Unfortunately, I still forgot important things. Time pressures overwhelm, and stress contributed to the problem.

One day a few years ago, I was telling my family how upset I was that my e-mail newsletter went out with a bad link in it. Hundreds of people let me know about the mistake. It took hours to straighten out a problem that could have so easily been avoided. My son, a pilot, immediately jumped in to ask if I had a checklist. I looked at him like he was nuts, then countered that I was a professional, not a McDonald's employee. My work was sophisticated and couldn't be easily encapsulated in a checklist. He stood firm, telling me that pilots always use checklists, even the most experienced ones.

Since that time, my marketing director has created a newsletter checklist that we now use religiously before we hit "Send" on a newsletter. We haven't had problems since then. It didn't take long for me to become a real fan of checklists. I loved how they freed up my memory for the more important things. Checklists also ensure that you don't unwittingly make stupid mistakes.

Here's one I recently created for online video meetings. Before I hold one, I make sure I've checked off every element on this list.

ONLINE MEETING CHECKLIST

Preparation

☐ De-clutter my work area.

☐ Turn up lights, avoiding windows behind me.

☐ Adjust camera so it's at eye level.

☐ Test equipment (camera, slides, microphone) to ensure that it works.

☐ Log on five minutes prior to meeting.

☐ Use headset to eliminate background noise.

☐ Shut down e-mail, instant messaging, and other distractions.

☐ Position myself in center of screen, three feet from computer.

☐ Turn on webcam.

☐ Move meeting viewer window to center to ensure eye contact.

☐ Press "Record" when meeting starts.

During Meeting

☐ Look into camera, smile, and welcome people when they log on.

☐ Begin with intros and a little chitchat.

☐ Review meeting purpose and time frames.

☐ Present vital, must-know information.

☐ Ask questions to gain insights and perspectives.

☐ Suggest/solicit input for logical next steps.

Follow Up

☐ Send e-mail confirming key points, decisions made, and "to dos."

☐ Forward recording to people who missed the meeting.

☐ Review meeting, looking for ways to improve skills.

What a godsend that checklist has been! I pull it out every time I do an online meeting, even though I've done hundreds of them. It's simple and I don't have to use one ounce of my limited brainpower to dwell on what materials or prep tasks are needed for the meeting. Instead, I'm able to focus on flawless execution.

As you're getting up to speed in your new job, think about what kinds of checklists you can create to simplify your life and ensure that you do things right. Here are some ideas for you:

- Pre-Call Research Checklist
- CRM (or any technology) Checklist
- Sales Proposal Checklist
- Lead Follow-up Checklist
- Sales Process Checklist
- Referral Checklist
- Messaging Checklist
- Key Questions Checklist
- Presentation Checklist
- RFP Preparation Checklist

- Contracting Checklist
- Negotiations Checklist
- Implementation Checklist

As you can see, there are countless jobs that you can simplify by creating a checklist. The key to creating a thorough, useful checklist is to document the steps you go through to complete a task or process. That's how you make your new job simple, simple, simple. Better yet, it increases your sales agility. Instead of having your brain all tied up trying to remember complex tasks, you'll be able to focus on higher-value activities related to sales strategies and buyer interactions.

> Make checklists to ensure
> you don't forget.

42

FIX THE ROOT CAUSE

Recently, I was on the phone with the key executives of a growing technology company. Just two weeks prior, I'd spoken at their sales kickoff meeting about how to get better at prospecting. We were talking about strategies they could implement to ensure that what their salespeople learned would stick.

With just ten minutes left on our call, Jeff, the sales VP, popped the question all sellers love to hear: "What should we be doing with you next, Jill?" Before I could say a word, Ginger, the regional sales manager, jumped in: "Closing skills. My team sucks at it. We lose way too many opportunities."

"Tell me more," I said. Ginger quickly rattled off three examples of forecasted sales they hadn't converted into clients. I had one last question for her: "Are you losing to competitors or did they decide to keep doing things the same old way?"

"They're not doing anything," Ginger responded. "And what makes it even worse, we've shown them all we've got. They've seen the demo. They've got a proposal. And still they're not budging."

"Seems to me that closing skills aren't the problem," I said.

"People won't buy unless they believe that changing is worthwhile. That's the real issue. No matter how much training your sales team gets on closing, it won't address the root cause of their problem."

Don't let yourself be fooled by symptoms. It's really easy to jump to an erroneous conclusion about what you need to change to get better results. You need to dig deeper to determine the root cause of the sales problems that you're personally facing. By changing your own behaviors and implementing different strategies, you can often realize fundamentally different results.

This problem-solving approach should help you figure out where you need to improve:

1. Identify potential causes. Most sellers immediately jump to one conclusion (for example, closing skills) and stop there. Expand your thinking beyond the obvious to find the root cause of the sales problems you've created by your actions. Ask: What's causing my sales problem? What else could be a cause of my problem? Create a list of potential factors.

2. Separate what you can control from what you can't. You don't have any impact on the economy or industry trends. But you have total control over what you do in every client interaction.

3. Sequence the factors. Now that you've identified the areas you can impact, look at their sequence in the sales cycle or sales meeting. In my experience, the root cause is often found much earlier in the sales journey than most people think. For example, closing problems are caused because prospects don't believe it makes sense to change. To solve them, the seller needs to focus on building a better busi-

ness case, not closing harder. Ask: Where is the true source of my problem?

4. Brainstorm solutions. Once you've identified the areas you can impact, brainstorm ways to address them. Perhaps you could ask better questions, develop a stronger ROI, delay pitching, or have a more engaging presentation. If you're stuck, go talk to other people who can offer you fresh insights. And finally, take action.

Every seller encounters problems. That's a given. How you handle them makes all the difference in the world. Agile sellers are open to exploring many more options than average sellers. Because of this, they're much more likely to identify and solve the root cause of their problems rather than the presenting symptom.

> Solve the right problem; don't let symptoms lead you astray.

43

TACKLE NEW TECHNOLOGY

Getting up to speed quickly is challenging enough. When you have to learn new technology on top of it, it can truly drive you up a wall. In every sales job, some technologies are a given, including your CRM or e-mail. You have to get up and running on them from day one. Other technologies—such as Skype, GoToMeeting, LinkedIn, and so many others—are add-ons.

For some, learning how to use technology is effortless. For people like me, it's hard. If at all possible, I make it a point to get one-on-one training from a knowledgeable person. Certainly I'm capable of reading manuals, but I quickly get lost. Having human assistance slashes days off my learning curve.

The first thing you need to do in familiarizing yourself with any new technology is to prioritize. Find out which applications are the most critical for you to master first and get started learning them. If you're already familiar with similar technologies, a quick overview of how the new one is similar to or different from the one you know will often suffice to get you operational. You can learn the details later, on an as-needed basis.

If you're learning totally new technologies, use these rapid learning strategies to speed up your time to proficiency:

• Know why. Understanding the ultimate benefit you'll realize helps make the learning curve more tolerable. Will it make you more productive? Deepen customer insights? Increase your conversion rates?

• Chunk. Find out what's essential to master first or what it takes to do a key task that's important for your business. Recently I took it upon myself to learn a new presentation software with countless capabilities. I chose to first focus on delivering voice-over proposals to geographically dispersed buyers. Now that I've got that down pat, I'll be moving on to YouTube applications. Doing one thing at a time develops proficiency and confidence.

• Observe. Ask your trainer (whether a colleague or IT specialist) to go through the entire process first, explaining what they're doing and why. That gives you the big-picture overview of what you're going to be learning as well as the sequence of steps.

• Do it together. After observing the pro use the program, it's your turn to try. Have your trainer tell you what to do at each step of the process. You need to take notes too; otherwise you'll forget things. (This is a great time to create a checklist.)

• Do it alone. Repeat the process, this time trying to do it all yourself. Your trainer's role is to watch and provide feedback if needed. Keep this up until you "get it."

• Conduct practice sessions. This is especially important with any customer-interfacing technologies (such as GoToMeeting or WebEx). You want to be a pro when you're with your prospects. If possible, get your trainer or colleagues involved in your tests.

Although trainers can give you a quick-start introduction to the technology, over the years I've learned that it's essential to rein trainers in. They just love to show you multiple ways you can accomplish the same task. All that does is screw you up and you don't remember anything. Now I always ask my trainers for the simplest way to do things.

You may also want to consider using video tutorials. In the absence of human assistance, they can be so useful. I frequently watch the step-by-step lessons multiple times in my learning process. Often the developer of the given program will have these training modules on its Web site. If not, you can also do a search for "tutorial + [name of technology]" and you're likely to find lots of resources, including videos, PDFs, guides, and checklists.

Finally, when you're learning new technology, you'll want to engage in real-time use on a daily or weekly basis. It's imperative to do this because otherwise, what you learned will totally disappear from your memory bank. Once you're fairly versed in one technology, it's time to tackle another one. Don't let yourself stop learning. It does get easier. By following these strategies, even technophobes like me can become competent users.

> Learn new technology deliberately:
> chunk, observe, practice, repeat.

44

STRIVE FOR MAXIMUM IMPACT

As a seller, you stand between your company's offering and the buyer's needs. To do your job well, you become an analyst, trend watcher, researcher, interpreter, evangelist, problem solver, relationship builder, guide, project manager, and more. You also need to be quick on the uptake, flexible in your thinking, and able to change directions when needed. Your knowledge, insights, and ideas are what differentiate you from everyone else.

In this book, we've already gone through numerous strategies to help you get up to speed quickly in your new sales position. But the reality is, you're never done learning about any of these topics. Top sellers spend more time prepping for meetings than average sellers, at every point in their careers. They still role-play. They debrief regularly. They exchange ideas with their colleagues.

Most important, top sellers experiment—all the time. High-performing agile sellers go for maximum impact in every interaction. That means that every single time they're talking to or working with a potential buyer, they want it to end with the best possible outcome.

When prospecting, they're always thinking about new ways to increase their effectiveness. They may experiment with different e-mail subject lines, first sentences, salutations, and messages. When giving presentations, these sellers think backward from their desired outcome, mapping out what has to happen to get there. They use negative thinking to ferret out potential land mines. Then they think creatively about how to avoid or handle those situations.

Top sellers are also intensely perceptive about their prospects. Before they meet, they review their meeting plan from their customer's perspective. Is it relevant? Focused on a priority? Does it flow well? Is it complex or simple to understand? During the meeting, they're looking out for clues about their prospect's true thinking, as well as checking in to make sure.

The more you think in sales, the better you get at it. The more you learn, the more resources you have at your disposal. The more you experiment, the better your success rate. The better your thinking, the more agile you are in sales meetings. It's definitely a positive trend line to be on.

Also, by embracing a maximum-impact philosophy, you can achieve your goals with fewer prospects, minimal competition, and in less time. You'll also get more business from your existing customers. That's something we should all strive for.

Constantly ask yourself: "How can I have maximum impact?" When you do, you'll stay on the path to getting better. And as we learned, focusing on getting better is a mastery mind-set.

Focus on maximum impact to achieve
the best possible outcomes.

Part 5

Success Habits of

Agile Sellers

Staying agile is crucial for long-term success.
Use these success habits on an as-needed basis
to sharpen your skills, keep motivated, recover
from setbacks, and better manage your time.

45

PREPARE FOR SUCCESS

We're in the home stretch. So far, you've learned about the mind-set that's crucial for sales success. You know how important it is to make a commitment to success, turn problems into challenges, and failure-proof yourself. You've learned many strategies to quickly become knowledgeable about your products, services, and customers. And you've discovered what it takes to learn selling skills as fast as humanly possible.

It's time to turn our attention to success habits—those things you can do on a daily or as-needed basis to ensure you're at the top of your game. In this section, you'll find numerous strategies to:

- Maximize your productivity so you get more done in less time.
- Keep going when you're buckling under pressure to perform.

- Expand your options and creative thinking when you're stuck.
- Create a work environment that makes it easier to reach your goals.

Some of these strategies are firmly rooted in research from within the sales profession, while others come from studies that have direct impact on sellers. I've also included some tools and tactics that I've personally implemented over the years that have made a big difference for me and everyone I've shared them with.

Nailing down these success habits is the final cornerstone on your path to sales proficiency. Paying attention here ensures optimal performance. After all, you don't want to get bogged down in behaviors and habits that hurt your chances of success.

So dig in and look for tidbits that resonate with you right now. You can implement these right away, then come back for more whenever you need a refresher or a kick in the butt, or when you're ready for the next step.

> Failure-proof your sales habits and thinking.

46

PUT THIS PLAN IN PLACE

The best way to ensure you get off to a good start in your new position, as we covered, is to take charge of your own learning. Don't ever leave it to someone else. Even if your company has a top-notch training program, it doesn't cover everything. But beyond that, learning how to be an agile seller is really about personal accountability.

The best way to be accountable to your own learning schedule is to create a 90-Day Plan that covers exactly what you need to learn. This time frame is short enough to feel manageable, yet long enough to get results.

Here is a simplified 90-Day Plan that will give you an idea about what could be included in your learning schedule:

Weeks 1 and 2

Complete company-specific training (for example, products, sales, and industry).

Map out and prioritize "need to know" now info necessary for situational credibility.

Immerse yourself in relevant product knowledge and marketplace.

Begin to fill out Buyer's Matrix on primary buyers.

Create dictionary, cheat sheets, and checklists to aid recall.

Map out decision process, getting clear on all buyer's steps.

Clarify primary status quos and business case for making a change.

Get up to speed on technology needed to do job.

Start collecting customer stories; learn the difference you make.

Weeks 3 and 4

Continue buyer and product immersions, going into greater depth.

Take the gobbledygook test to ensure clarity in your presentations.

Contact and set up conversations with priority customers.

Tap into colleagues' expertise to include:

    Effective prospecting strategies

    Interviews with upstarts and seasoned pros

    Listening in on phone conversations

    Field travel and other sales-related opportunities

Develop targeted prospecting list, research decision makers, and launch prospecting initiative.

Invest time prepping for meetings.

Role-play all new sales activities to ensure that you're ready for prime time.

30–60 Days

Continue working on above, deepening knowledge and expertise in "need to know" now areas.

Identify primary trigger events to leverage in prospecting.

Review key accounts to flush out opportunities and issues; develop and begin implementing strategy to solidify relationship.

Fine-tune prospecting approach, looking for ways to increase effectiveness.

Develop a strong game plan for initial conversations.

Expand knowledge of your company, sales resources, and helpful people.

Leverage technology to record info, conduct research on customers, and communicate with customers.

Invest time prepping for meetings and role-playing new sales skills.

Debrief after important calls; identify areas for improvement.

Observe colleagues in action; identify potential role models.

60–90 Days

Continue working on above, expanding knowledge beyond "need to know" now areas.

Add more prospects to pipeline, while at the same time advancing existing prospects through the decision process.

Improve sales productivity to ensure optimal time in high-payback sales activities.

Expand contacts in key accounts, resolve issues, propose new ideas; interview customers to learn more about their processes and the business value you can provide.

Track and monitor activity to identify areas for improvement.

Join one relevant trade association and attend its meetings.

Please realize that your 90-Day Plan may be different from this one. It all depends on factors such as what you sell, how much training you get, your experience level, the length of your sales cycle, and company support.

Make sure to include a weekly conversation with your boss in this 90-Day Plan too. You'll want to continually clarify expectations, discuss your progress, review opportunities, brainstorm strategies, and improve skills with your higher-ups.

Being accountable to your own learning cycle is an agility habit that allows you to track your own progress and manage any new role.

> Create a learning plan to expedite
> your professional development.

47

POWER-PACK YOUR DAY

When you're new, there's never enough time in a day to get everything done. No matter how hard you try, you'll accomplish only a fraction of the things you'd hoped to do. That's why it's imperative to wisely use the limited hours at your disposal. Unfortunately, because most sellers start their day by checking e-mail and logging into their CRM system, they've immediately started their day on the wrong foot.

How could these two seemingly innocuous tasks create problems? Believe it or not, e-mail is a real brain drain. Each message requires thinking; many require responses. Doing this for thirty to forty-five minutes bogs you down, zaps your best ideas, and ensures that other people's priorities are met instead of your own. To make matters worse, your CRM's daily to-do list can't differentiate what's really important from the trivial.

To ensure that you get the right work done in the shortest possible time—and as soon as possible—try the following strategies for power-packing your day:

Prioritize daily. Prioritize the day's activities first thing in the morning when your brain is fresh. According to David Rock, author of *Your Brain at Work,* "prioritizing is one of the brain's most energy-hungry resources. Even after just a few mental activities, you may not have the resources left to prioritize."

Start by writing down the three or four most important things you need to get done that day. Then figure out the sequence in which you should execute these tasks. Always, always tackle your most important priority first. That way, no matter what happens, you'll have made progress on your crucial business. Prioritizing also requires being disciplined about what you *won't* think about today. You don't want to waste your precious time on nonessentials.

Chunk your time. This is so darn important, yet it's a strategy that few sellers use effectively. You should think in blocks of thirty-, sixty-, or ninety-minute intervals, max. Any longer is counterproductive.

During those time blocks, do only one activity. Make prospecting calls. Work on proposals. Research companies. Strategize on key accounts. When you focus on one task at a time, you get into a state of flow. Your brain is firing on all cylinders, totally in the zone, which enables you to get so much more done in the limited amount of time.

I've also found it really helps to chunk time related to specific sales opportunities. For example, after talking to a good prospect on the phone, I'll dedicate the next thirty minutes to consolidating my notes, fleshing out how I can offer value, and writing a draft of the discussion document I want to use in our next conversation. By doing this right away, I come up with much better ideas and I don't waste time later, trying to refresh my memory.

Another way to chunk time is around prospecting. It's

highly likely that it'll take you eight to ten contact attempts before you finally get a conversation set up with a prospect. That means you'll be writing lots of e-mails and/or calling. If you've just invested lots of time researching a targeted account, it's a good use of your time to actually map out your entire account entry campaign at once. Write four or five e-mails and a few phone messages. Pull it all together at one time and then just start implementing. You can almost put your prospecting on cruise control.

Set deadlines. According to Parkinson's Law, work expands to fill the time available for its completion. Most of us grossly overestimate how long a task can take when we're focused on it. If you doubt this, look at how much you can get done at work just before you go on vacation!

If it takes you half an hour to get your e-mail done each morning, give yourself fifteen minutes instead to complete the task. If you normally spend three hours researching a company, slash the time in half and tell yourself that's the only time you'll get. You'll be amazed at the results, and better yet, free up lots of time for more important tasks.

You don't need to work eight days a week to be successful. But you do need to use your available work hours to the best advantage.

> Control your schedule;
> don't let it control you.

48

PURGE THE PIPELINE

It was Monday morning and Ron, one of my sales reps, was in my office reviewing his sales forecast with me. Although I'd been a sales manager at Xerox for only a short time, I was beginning to notice a disconcerting trend. For the third month in a row, Ron was projecting that he'd close the same prospects he'd been unable to close the previous month.

When I asked him about it, he said, "They want a new system, Jill. They told me so. They're hoping to move ahead any time now." When I challenged his thinking, he vehemently disagreed. Yet the truth is, less than 20 percent of those prospects ever turned into customers.

Hope is rampant in sales. We need it to keep going—but we also need to avoid being fooled by false hope. The longer a deal stays in your pipeline, the less likely you are to ever close it, even if your prospect claimed that he or she desperately needed your offering. If the sales process does get stalled out, the only person who loses is you.

Purging your pipeline regularly keeps you honest with yourself. To do so, get in touch with your long-term prospects to see what's happening. Find out if they're still serious about making a change, and if so, realistically when. If they're hemming and hawing about when they'll change, they're not a prospect right now. If they tell you other, more urgent priorities have emerged, they're not going to be buying in the near future. If they tell you that the boss isn't sold, it's not likely you'll get a signed contract anytime soon.

You'll want to keep in touch if they're still interested but projecting significant delays—but don't count on them. If they don't respond to your calls or e-mails, take them off your prospect list right now. Don't delude yourself into thinking they'll close.

Learning to let go is an invaluable skill in this business. It keeps you realistic about the opportunities (or lack of them) in front of you. It frees up mental energy to pursue new prospects that you have a better chance of winning. It keeps you agile.

Take ten minutes right now to review that pipeline. Don't be afraid of the purge.

> Don't fool yourself about your chances of closing stalled deals.

49

DIG UP MORE DIRT

With all the great resources available today, there's no excuse for not knowing about your prospect, their company, and their industry, and possessing rock-solid business acumen.

If you still need more information, take the initiative and find people in your own company who can help you fill in any gaps in your learning. Your objective is to get answers. Tell your colleagues what you're trying to find out. Ask them who has the information you need. Set up meetings with these people and plan your specific questions so that you can make the best use of your time.

Picking colleagues' brains is just a starting point. There's a wealth of great information available online that can help you get up to speed pretty darn fast. It all starts with doing some good searches with multiple criteria like this: "wholesale distributors" + trends or "research – computers." Please note the use of quotes to help you find exact phrases, plus signs to add criteria, minus signs to exclude terms, and the use of "or" when words are interchangeable. This is important, because the quality of your search dictates the quality of your search results.

Also, check out the following types of Web sites. They're often filled with great information. You can swoop in for some quick insights and also monitor them on a regular basis. Constant vigilance is good. As you do your research, look for common themes to help you identify what's most important to your prospects today.

- Associations: Just about every single job position (for example, payroll managers, electrical engineers, CFOs) and field (medical devices, law firms, teachers) has a related association. These Web sites are filled with rich information on what's happening in the industry. Sign up for newsletters. Check out upcoming webinars. Watch the videos. Specifically look for trends and changing regulations because they alert you to trigger events.

- Consultants/Analysts: There are experts who support, advise, or evaluate virtually every industry. These individuals and their organizations often spread their expertise in multiple formats: articles, e-books, videos, podcasts, white papers. One good site can provide you with a complete education about a given field.

- Bloggers: Look for industry-related blogs written by passionate individuals who love to share their expertise. Read through their posts to see if you find good stuff. If so, sign up to get updates. If not, move on.

- Business News Sites: To develop overall business acumen, check out Forbes.com, Fortune.com, wsj.com, and other similar sites. Visit them regularly so you can deepen your business knowledge or at least find out what you need to learn next.

- Competitive Sites: By visiting the Web sites of your own

company's primary competitors, you'll learn about their offerings and positioning. Make sure you read any relevant white papers, e-books, or articles. If they have any upcoming online events that are open to the public, consider signing up too. You'll learn a lot about not only their positioning, but how you stack up against the competition, point by point.

• Trade Press: Virtually every industry and market sector has its own magazine. You can learn about industry news, hot issues, key players, and more. You'll get a broader perspective because the publisher can put things in context for you.

• Social Media: Don't overlook Twitter, Facebook, and other forms of social media. Follow heavy hitters and companies, track industry hash tags, and participate in conversations. Check out what they're recommending.

• Books: For a comprehensive overview of a given field, a book might be the best starting place. Beginners might find it useful to check out the Dummies or Idiot series books on nearly any topic. You can also find books that specialize in certain industries, technologies, careers, and more.

There's no shortage of information out there. But in reality, few sellers invest in self-education. Those who do invariably outperform the ones who try to take the shortcuts. Today's buyers suffer no fools, so make sure you get smart.

> Keep developing your expertise;
> it sets you apart.

50

ELIMINATE DISTRACTIONS

I t's obvious that your time is not an unlimited resource, but you probably don't know just how much your time is worth. If you haven't figured out your hourly income, do so right now. It'll help you understand why minimizing distractions is so crucial.

Distractions are not just a hassle. They significantly hinder our ability to get up to speed quickly. In *Information Overload: We Have Met the Enemy and He Is Us,** the authors state that distractions consume an average of 2.1 hours per day. Even with a minor distraction, it can take a significant amount of time to get back on track. Studies say that it can take five to twenty-five minutes to return to the task at hand after an interruption such as a phone call, a colleague stopping by, or even a quick game of solitaire (my downfall) on your computer.

Distractions stress you out too, and when that happens, cortisol (hormone) is released, making it more difficult to concen-

* *Information Overload* is a report highlighting research by Basex.com.

trate. Your memory, great sales ideas, and keen insights can disappear in a nanosecond.

Here are some very practical strategies you can implement to prevent distractions from screwing up your day:

• Put away unrelated work. Personally, I've found this to be essential. When I'm struggling to learn new skills or information, I can easily be seduced by virtually any distraction. The only way I can keep on task is to clear my desk of any unrelated files or piles that could capture my attention.

• Close your door. If you have your own office, you have to keep people out if you're going to concentrate. If you find that people are still knocking and popping their head in, add a "Do Not Disturb" sign. If it makes you feel better, write when you'll be available on the sign.

• Wear headphones. If you're sharing space with lots of other people, wearing headphones is often the equivalent of a "Do Not Disturb" sign. If you still get frequent interruptions, tape a sign to your back. Have a sense of humor about it!

• Move to a different area. As I write this, I'm in a coffee shop. It's the perfect way for me to have alone time, even though I'm in the midst of a group of people. If you work in an office, go to a conference room—preferably far away from your colleagues.

• Say no. How often do colleagues or supervisors walk by and interrupt with "Got a few minutes?" If these kinds of distractions are frequent, you need to ask, "Is it critical to talk now or can it wait for ninety minutes?" The truth is, most things can wait. For some, this tactic may seem rude—but your time is valuable and even a short interruption can have a negative impact on getting your work done.

• Create a parking lot. Of course, you can't clear all distractions definitively. There's no way your brain won't wander—even when you're trying to concentrate on one specific task. What I've learned to do is write all my wandering ideas down quickly on a Post-it note so I don't forget them. Then I immediately get back to what I'm working on.

- Don't answer the phone. For a salesperson, this may seem like heresy. After all, your best prospect could be calling in to give you the go-ahead. I know you want to be there for your customers, but they don't expect you to be there 24/7 for them.

Eliminating these distractions can dramatically increase your productivity at the same time it reduces stress levels. You'll get into the flow, learn faster, and be successful in your new job much sooner.

> Take charge of your environment
> to keep distractions at bay.

51

UPGRADE YOUR BRAIN

To get up to speed quickly, every ounce of your brainpower is needed to assimilate all that new information and learn all those new skills. That's why it's essential to tackle bad habits you have that are severely affecting your abilities. One of the worst offenders? Multitasking.

You probably don't even know how much this bad habit hurts you. After all, would you willingly engage in behavior that makes you dumber? Yet, according to a study by Dr. Glenn Wilson of the University of London, that's exactly what happens when we multitask. Constant e-mail and texting reduces your mental capacity significantly. Women's IQ scores dropped an average of 5 percent. For men, multitasking was catastrophic: Their IQ dropped fifteen points.

Research by Harold Pashler, a University of California, San Diego, scientist who studies "dual-task interference," also supports that finding. His studies show that when people do two cognitive tasks at once, their intellectual capacity can drop from that of a Harvard MBA to an eight-year-old.

Ouch! That's serious mental degradation. Yet we've erroneously come to the belief that multitasking enables us to get more done in less time when it's actually the opposite. According to a study published by the American Psychological Association, it takes you 20 to 40 percent more time to get your work done when you're multitasking. When you're learning new information, it's much closer to the 40 percent level.

Those product highlights and buyer insights just don't want to stick in your memory if you're trying to do something else at the same time. When you try to recall them later, everything you thought you learned is gone because the information hasn't made it into your long-term memory. This poor integration means you'll end up making more mistakes in your information recall and skill development.

I'm as guilty of falling into the multitasking trap as anyone: While I'm talking to someone on the phone or listening to a webinar, I'm constantly checking my e-mail. I literally have to remind myself that multitasking doesn't work; I won't remember what I heard and, overall, I'll waste more time.

Here are three things I've been working on to prevent myself from multitasking. Try them out:

Check e-mail on a schedule. Pick three or four times per day when you allow yourself to review the messages that come in and respond to them. The lure of e-mail is strong. And, as a seller, you have this incredible urge to see if anything new is happening. But remember, constantly checking it will make you way less productive—and you'll screw up on the things you are doing.

Protect yourself from yourself. Like many, I jump from one activity to the other, even though I know better. Recently, I've started using technology to prevent me from suc-cumbing to my own impulses. For example, as I'm writing this, I'm using a Word function called Focus (under View) that lets me see only this document. The rest of my screen is blacked out. I also use Anti-Social, an app that blocks me from going to my personal time-wasting sites or keeps me off-line alto-gether for a designated period of time. When I seriously want to get things done on time, this is an ideal solution.

Totally disconnect. I know it's hard to do this when you're in sales, but seriously there are times when you just need to think. Turn off your devices entirely so they can't interrupt you. Ninety minutes of time in which you're totally focused on learning your new knowledge and skills will get you up to speed faster than anything else.

Multitasking is out. Today, we need to start bragging about our ability to monotask. It's a sign of intelligence and compe-tence.

> Eliminate multitasking to learn
> faster and think better.

52

OPTIMIZE YOUR ATTITUDE

'll never forget the day that Karen, a new rep, walked into my office, reeking of discouragement. "Boss," she said. "People don't care about how good Xerox is. I might as well be selling wastebaskets." After just three months, she chose to take a different job. To me, the saddest part was that she left feeling like a failure.

It's amazing what a difference your attitude can make, for better or for worse. In his book *Drive: The Surprising Truth About What Motivates Us,* Daniel Pink writes: "The science shows that the secret to high performance isn't our biological drive or our reward-and-punishment drive, but our third drive—our deep-seated desire to direct our own lives, to expand and extend our abilities, and to live a life of purpose." Top sellers want to know that what they do matters. In *Selling with Noble Purpose,* Lisa Earle McLeod shares what she found in her six-year study of top performers: "Salespeople who sell with noble purpose—who want to make a difference to customers—outsell salespeople who focus on sales goals and money."

Clearly Karen felt like what she was doing didn't matter; she

didn't connect with that third drive or recognize her noble purpose. Unfortunately, because she was so disheartened, I couldn't
help her see the difference she was making. That's why so much
of Part 3 is focused on helping you understand the value of what
you sell. My experience shows me that when salespeople "get"
the impact of their products or services, they're much more persistent. In short, knowing your value makes you more resilient
when things don't go the way you'd hoped. When you're feeling
down, purpose is what allows you to snap yourself out of a funk
by focusing on how you help your customers.

Steve had a slightly different attitude problem. He was a top-
performing rep whose sales had plummeted in the past few
months. When we talked about the slump, he kept saying that
the recession was killing him. Yet when I spent a day making
sales calls with him, it became abundantly clear to me why he
was struggling—he started virtually every sales meeting by asking his prospects: "So, how's the recession impacting your business?" The conversation just went downhill from there. No
wonder he was discouraged.

We talked about how his attitude was the root cause of the
problem and brainstormed ways to deal with the issue. Steve
took it to heart and immediately changed what he was doing.
Just three months later, he'd made up his year-to-date shortfall
and earned the Sales Rep of the Month award, beating out forty-
five other reps.

What happened here? For one thing, when Steve took some
time to reflect on what we talked about, he decided it was worthwhile to experiment with an optimistic approach for both himself and his prospects. The optimism itself created change. In a
study of new hire agents at MetLife, the optimists outsold the
pessimists by 31 percent. That's significant.

Optimism can be learned or controlled; essentially, if you're feeling down, you can change your feelings. It all goes back to realizing that despite how bad things seem, there are always factors you can control. You can transform the problem into a challenge. You can turn the failure into a learning experience. You can look for the positives within the difficulties.

That's precisely what Steve did and it made all the difference in the world. He didn't wake up blindly optimistic the next day. He didn't try to improve his self-esteem by repeating meaningless affirmations like "I am a wonderful sales guy. I deserve to have lots of sales." Instead, he focused on optimizing his attitude every day, sometimes multiple times a day. Whenever fear, uncertainty, or doubt reared their ugly faces, he stared them down, refusing to let them win.

You can do the same. In fact, make it a success habit of yours.

> Change your attitude if it's impacting your sales.

53

TEACH SOMEONE A LESSON

Maybe it's time you teach someone a lesson. Hey—I'm not talking about being vindictive or seeking revenge! There may be some people who elicit that feeling in you, but we're not going to go there. Instead, we're going to focus on a super simple but highly effective strategy with big payback for you: teaching others in order to solidify your own knowledge.

The first time I ever trained someone else was early in my first year of sales. My boss, Diane, instructed me to go on a sales call with Alice, a trainee who had uncovered a really good sales opportunity while prospecting. As a newbie, it was highly unlikely that she'd close the deal without assistance. Diane asked me to show Alice what to do and to make sure we got the business.

Aargh! I was not ready for that. I was still fairly new myself, plus I didn't know much about the other vendors. But clearly coming in second was not an option. For the next two days, I immersed myself in learning everything I could about the other two competitors. I studied how they stacked up against us. I talked to experienced reps to find out about pricing. Finally, I planned out how I'd engage the prospect in a conversation that made us the obvious choice.

Before we went to the meeting, I reviewed everything with Alice. I outlined competitive strengths and weaknesses. I overviewed our plan for the meeting. I answered her questions to the best of my knowledge. With that prep, Alice and I went to the prospect's office. Two hours later, we walked out with a signed contract. I was never so relieved in my whole life.

Here's what closed that deal: I took a crash course in two competitors and became an overnight expert. In order to teach Alice, I had to really think through my meeting strategy step-by-step. Then I had to figure out how to explain to her what I was going to do in the meeting and why. Because I wanted to look good in front of Alice, my boss, and the prospect, I actually leapfrogged in my own sales development.

It seems strange to recommend teaching others while you're still learning yourself. After all, we so quickly defer to the experts. However, the upside can be huge. As the Roman philosopher Seneca wrote nearly two thousand years ago, "By teaching, we learn."

Annie Murphy Paul, author of *Brilliant: The New Science of Smart,* writes about a program at the University of Pennsylvania in which students are responsible for teaching a specific subject to a computerized character. She writes, "As they prepare to teach, they organize their knowledge, improving their own understanding and recall." Doing this helps them find gaps in their own learning too, and they're more motivated to master the material.

That's exactly what happened to me. Teaching really challenged me to learn quickly. I felt really good about it. Alice learned. I got better. Consequently, we got the order that day.

After Alice, I had a string of trainees at Xerox. Each one increased my skill level. I became a conscious competent about what I was doing. In other words, I knew what worked, but it wasn't second nature to me yet. Doing it right required me to pay close attention to all the steps involved. By teaching, I accelerated my learning significantly.

To this day, I teach so I can learn. You might want to give it a try. Think about what you really want to (or need to) learn about in more depth right now. What is it? Who could you teach it to? It doesn't have to be people in your own company. Get creative. But most of all, start teaching so you learn faster.

> Accelerate your own learning
> by teaching others.

54

GAMING THE SYSTEM

On your mark. Get set. Go!

That's exactly how this chapter began. Right now, I'm playing the Beat the Clock game. I've given myself ninety minutes to create the initial draft. Normally, I agonize over each chapter for at least a day. But this time, I allotted thirty minutes to watch a gamification video, thirty minutes to review research and go over my notes, and thirty minutes to write. I'm under pressure to get it done. My thoughts are coming together . . . I need to start writing . . . Here we go!

I've been a gamer since I started in sales. I kept creating all these little games to play with myself. They motivated me, but I always felt a little silly playing them. That is, until I recently learned that neuroscience research has discovered that games activate the brain's "seeking circuit." In other words, they create challenges that our brains just can't resist.

The best games to play are right at the edge of your skill level. They test what you're learning and help you master things far faster than traditional learning. Here are some of my personal favorites:

The Objection Game. Whenever I encounter an objection that stumps me, I turn it into a game. For example, I hate it when prospects say, "I'm not interested," especially when I know I could really help them out. Clearly something I said elicited that response—but what? To find out the answer, I replay as best I can what I was talking about just prior to their reaction. Then I try to figure out how to say things differently, so that my next prospect will say, "Ooh, that's interesting. Tell me more." When I get that response, I win. It's tougher to do than you might imagine; I've spent days thinking and rethinking how to get a different reaction. Sometimes it's required me to rethink my entire approach. But I love winning this one.

The Competitive Game. When I'm up against a known competitor, I approach it like a chess game. I ask myself questions like "What moves are they likely to make? How can I gain an advantage? Where are my weaknesses?" Looking at my ability to close a deal as a zero-sum game spurs my thinking. I'm not just going through the motions; I'm actually challenged to my maximum.

The One-Customer Game. In this game, I take a look at my best customer and ask, "If this were the only company I could work with, what would I need to do to earn a decent living here?" This game has serious parameters, which make it even more challenging. To win, you have to ask lots of questions like: Where else could I go in this organization? Which of our products/services aren't they using? How can I change that? How can I leverage existing relationships for more business? How can I keep competitors out? This game is fun. Playing it enabled me to sell significantly more to my key customer—and it was so much easier than having to prospect for the same volume of business.

Some of these games might sound silly on the surface, but they work. Games turn chores into fun and get you excited about your work. They encourage exploration and creativity. Games also engage your brain in an iterative process, testing and trying new things, so they're the perfect setups for developing learning agility.

As human beings, we're built to learn this way. And we can reward ourselves every time we accomplish our objectives. That's part of the fun too. Perhaps you can treat yourself to a coffee break, a day off, or lunch at your favorite restaurant. Bigger or riskier games might have higher payoffs. I recently rewarded myself with a nice shopping spree—and no, I'm not telling you what I did to earn it!

So start thinking. What can you turn into a game today? Perhaps you can create one that helps you learn all that info about your new company faster. Or how about setting up a sales game that tests you on the skills that you're working on improving? It's a great way to learn faster.

(Remember how I said I played the Beat the Clock game to write this chapter? In case you're wondering, this entire exercise took ninety-two minutes.)

> Play games to stretch beyond
> your current capabilities.

55

CHANGE SABOTAGING BEHAVIORS

don't intentionally do things to reduce my chances of success.
Yet, if I'm honest with myself, I've developed some pretty bad
habits that are doing just that. It became readily apparent to
me recently when I did an audit of how I spent my working time.
For one week, I wrote down what I was doing every fifteen
minutes—uncensored.

When I reviewed the log on Friday afternoon, I was embarrassed. Although I'd been at my desk since eight A.M., I didn't
really get started on my work until ten A.M. As a night owl, I
justified that behavior for years. However, seeing it down on
paper made it clear that I was totally wasting way too many
mornings. I was constantly behind and forcing myself to work
evenings and weekends to catch up. That's no way to live.

After reading Charles Duhigg's *The Power of Habit,* I learned
some interesting things about how we develop patterns in our
lives. Most of what we do each day is simply a habit in which our
brain strings a sequence of actions together into an automatic

routine. For the most part, this unconscious activity is a good thing because it frees up mental resources for more important tasks. But sometimes our habits become saboteurs, either hurting us or limiting our potential.

Duhigg says that understanding a habit's anatomy is crucial for change. Each habit has a cue, a routine, and a reward. So here was my morning habit that was killing me:

> **Cue:** Getting out of bed.
>
> **Routine:** After that, I washed up, got dressed, made coffee, ate a quick bite, and then plopped down at my computer for a couple of hours as I checked my e-mail, read the news, and reviewed nonessential material until my brain kicked in.
>
> **Reward:** Cups of my favorite coffee.

I wanted to stop wasting my morning hours but, as research shows, you can't just will it into happening. Your habits are powerful. They rule how you operate. Despite all your good intentions, before long you're back to the same old bad practices. You need to deliberately plan to change a habit.

According to Duhigg's Golden Rule of Habit Change, to get different results you need to "Use the same cue. Provide the same reward. Change the routine." That's exactly what I did. Now, after getting up (same cue), I have a new routine: While I'm washing up, I drink a tall glass of water with a lemon in it. Then I get dressed in workout clothes, lace up my sneakers, turn on the coffeepot, and head out for a one- to two-mile walk. Essentially my normal cue triggers a different—and better— routine. When I get back, I fill up my coffee cup (same reward), grab a quick bite to eat, and then get to work.

Believe it or not, exercising as soon as I get up changed everything about how I work. I can actually think now in the morning. More work is getting done during my work hours. And I've got more free time.

I know I'm not the only one who has sabotaged my success. I suspect you have a few unhelpful habits too. Perhaps you could start by taking a look at your prospecting habits. For example, let's say that the first thing you do each morning is to sit down at your desk (cue) and compile a list of everyone you want to contact that day. Then your habit kicks in as you begin your follow-up. If you're like most sellers, I'd be surprised if your message didn't begin like this: "Hi, John. Just circling back (checking in, touching base) to see if you've had a chance to look at the information I sent." When you're done with everything, you reward yourself with a quick stroll around the office to chat with a few colleagues and grab a fresh cup of coffee.

What can you change? If not too many people are returning your calls, challenge yourself to create a different message that's more effective. You could try focusing more on the business case for making change. You could send a case study or the link to an educational (not promotional) article. You have lots of options. You just haven't explored or tested them yet.

In reality, much of selling is simply habit. We do the same things over and over again, often with results that we don't like. But instead of seeing what we're doing as a changeable habit, we make excuses or put the blame elsewhere.

I encourage you to be honest with yourself. What success-sabotaging behaviors do you have? Take a serious look at their cue, the routine you have in place, and the reward you're getting. Then change the routine for a new, ingrained habit that yields better results.

> Replace bad habits with ones that serve you better.

56

GET GRITTIER

Let's talk about those days or even weeks when you're so frustrated with how difficult it is to figure everything out. You're worried about quotas, or afraid that taking this sales job wasn't such a good career move.

Here's the brutal truth: You may be right. Not all companies are great, some bosses are jerks, and the training you get could very well be a joke. You may be nodding your head right now, saying, "That's it, Jill. That's my situation exactly. It's sink or swim here—and right now, I'm sinking."

Dreaming of a fresh start somewhere else sometimes feels a whole lot more appealing than facing up to the challenges in front of you. Before you do that, know this: Right now, your fears, uncertainties, and doubts are running the show. The gloom-and-doom scenario they're painting doesn't consider the fact that some salespeople (from your company or elsewhere) are successful with similar or inferior products or services. Or that other entrepreneurs, consultants, or freelancers with far less talent are making a go of it in the marketplace.

What are others doing to achieve success? Well, they've made that pivotal decision to figure it out. They're willing to do what it takes to wrestle their challenge to the ground. They're tenacious and persistent even in the face of insurmountable challenges.

This resilience is what University of Pennsylvania psychology professor Angela Duckworth calls "grit," which I think is a perfect word for it. According to her research, grit is a much greater predictor of professional success than a person's innate intelligence or talents. The good news is that you're born with a certain level of grit. With practice, you can develop your tolerance, resilience, and, of course, your agility.

Turning problems into challenges makes you grittier. So does reframing failure as a valuable learning experience. Setting "getting better" goals helps too. What's really important is to make grit a personal success habit—one you leverage whenever you face adversity.

Here are some ways you can build more grit:

Focus on what's controllable. What's important from the get-go is separating the areas you can impact from those you can't. Then you need to deliberately make a choice to not spend one iota of your precious time on areas you can't influence (for example, pricing, economy, marketing support). Instead, dedicate all your energy to areas that you can affect such as your skill level, depth of knowledge, how you spend your time, and your mind-set.

Challenge yourself. Pick a small habit you want to change, like delaying checking e-mail for an hour. Or, put yourself in an uncomfortable situation. I recently spoke out publicly about a sales-related issue that really bothered me—

and got significant flak for doing it. It was tough, but I'm stronger because of it. If you need to get grittier, I'd suggest you take risks on minor things before you tackle bigger ones. While you're challenging yourself, be conscious that you're building grit. Although it's not actually a muscle, grit acts like one; the more you use it, the stronger it gets.

Take a break. Research shows that grit is also a finite resource. When you're under intense pressure to perform and you're stressed out because of it, your stick-to-itiveness quickly evaporates. Recognize when your grit is waning and give yourself a breather. Take a walk, talk to friends, or play a game. Do something to refresh yourself for a short period of time. By taking the pressure off yourself, even momentarily, you refill your grit reserves and are better able to handle the stress.

Most of all, don't give up on yourself. Developing more grit makes a huge difference—not only to your success in your job today, but for your whole life.

> Develop your resilience by practicing grit-building exercises.

57

BORROW A BRAIN

Sometimes we just don't know enough or, worse yet, don't even know what we don't know. We're neophytes who lack the knowledge and skills to handle challenging situations or to take us to the next level. That's when things can get really tough for us—especially if we're on our own, unable to get guidance from a colleague.

Early on in my career, I bumped into a strategy that's provided big dividends for me over the years. In fact, just recently I leveraged it to negotiate a much bigger sponsorship contract than I ever thought was possible.

Here's how it all started. When I began my sales career at Xerox, I trained under Jim Farrell. He was a top-notch salesperson, masterful in his dealings with people, and incredibly street savvy. I hoped that someday I could achieve his level of competence.

After a few months, I finally got my own territory. I was scared. Now I had to do it on my own, and clearly, I was no Jim Farrell. As I was sitting in my car one day, trying to get up the gumption to cold-call, my mind was racing through all sorts of tough sales scenarios. What if the customer asked me about our new product and I didn't know the answer? What if they said they weren't interested? What if, what if, what if . . . ?

I was deep into catastrophizing when it hit me. I might not know how to respond, but Jim sure would. By thinking about how he'd react and using that as my guide, I could handle almost anything. From then on, when prospects asked questions I couldn't answer, instead of sounding like a babbling idiot, I parroted Jim: "Great question. Why is that important to you?" When they tried to dismiss me by saying they already had a copier, I brought in his cheekiness: "Of course you do. That's why I'm here."

"Borrowing" Jim's brain was a lifesaver for me. It allowed me to shift my perspective away from the angst that had paralyzed my thinking. Plus, it turned my problem into a question: How would Jim handle this? Suddenly my brain had an irresistible challenge to solve and immediately went to work. New ideas and answers quickly popped into my head, enabling me to deal with customer scenarios I feared.

Even though it worked, I was much too embarrassed to tell anyone (especially Jim) about my new strategy. I was sure they'd think I was nuts. That didn't stop me from doing it, though. Over the years, I've borrowed someone else's brain in virtually every single career move I've ever made.

Sometimes I've used my more experienced colleagues' brains. But when I really need to stretch my thinking, I'll get more creative. Over the years, I've tapped into the brains of Steve Jobs, Princess Diana, Mahatma Gandhi, a couple of presidents, and many of my customers. The ideas and insights I've gained have been extraordinarily helpful in discovering options I didn't even know existed.

Many years later, I learned that "brain borrowing" is an actual creative problem-solving approach used by innovation companies to shift perspective. Hillary Clinton used the strategy when she was acclimating to her new role as first lady. She'd constantly ask herself, "What would Eleanor Roosevelt do?"

Next time you're stumped by what to do, consider borrowing someone else's brain. It's a perfect strategy to use when you're developing the necessary confidence, knowledge, and skills to deal with unfamiliar or uncomfortable situations. It's almost like having an invisible sales coach with you at all times. Use it when you need fresh perspectives too. Don't let yourself be trapped by your own limited experience.

I love the quote by former U.S. president Woodrow Wilson, who said, "I not only use all the brains I have, but also all that I can borrow."

Whose brain are you going to borrow today?

Expand your options by thinking from another person's perspective.

58

FAKE IT TILL YOU MAKE IT

When you're selling, there are always going to be times when you want to appear more confident than you actually feel. Perhaps you're meeting with some senior executives from a big company that you'd love to land as a client. Maybe you're up against a formidable competitor who has beaten you before. Or you might need new prospects so badly that you're afraid you'll sound pathetic.

Sometimes, before big meetings, I'd get sick to my stomach with fear. Other times I'd dread picking up the phone to make a call. Fortunately, I stumbled onto a secret confidence booster. I'd sing a little song to myself, "I Whistle a Happy Tune." The lyrics, which tell you to "hold your head erect" and "strike a careless pose" worked miracles for me. I'd stand up straighter, feigning the posture and attitude of a real pro.

When I did this, people responded to me differently. My fake confidence increased their perception of my competence, which strangely enough made me feel confident. At that time, I had no idea why it worked, but I sure loved the results.

Recently, I learned about body language research being conducted by Harvard Business School professor Amy Cuddy. She's made some fascinating discoveries around the techniques of "power posing."

What's a power pose? Essentially, it's one that takes up lots of space and exudes confidence. Think of professional athletes who've just won a championship. Their arms are raised in victory, chest out and shoulders back. Think of Wonder Woman, standing tall with her chin high in the air, hands on hips, elbows out, and her feet shoulder width apart. Think of a high-level executive with his feet up on his desk, leaning back with his arms behind his head. This is the body language of a winner. It communicates competence, trustworthiness, and credibility.

Cuddy discovered that, more than just connoting strength and competence, holding these power poses for just two minutes actually changes your body chemistry. They cause your body to release hormones that increase your confidence levels at the same time as they inhibit production of stress-causing hormones.

The net result is that changing your posture leads to greater feelings of power and higher levels of self-assurance. That's exactly what happened to me when I sang my tune. I assumed a power pose and within minutes felt totally ready to deal with my challenges.

Cuddy's research also shows that a person's posture affects who gets picked and who's successful. Since that's what sales is about, physically faking confidence is another tool to add to your arsenal—especially when you're not feeling that way.

Here are some ideas on how you can do it:

- Prior to making an important call, stand up and assume a power pose.

- If you're waiting to go into a big meeting, stop by the restroom before it starts and assume a power pose in privacy!
- When you're sitting in a lobby, take over the chair. Spread out while you wait.
- While giving a presentation, stand tall and use bigger gestures. Think of someone you can emulate. Repeat a personal mantra that makes you feel more powerful.

You need just two minutes to kick your hormones into gear. When that happens, you'll exude more confidence and your stress levels will decrease. Not bad for such a mini-investment of your time.

I'm not suggesting you use this strategy in place of having a good strong knowledge base to work from. Faking it works best when you need that extra edge; it gives you an irresistible aura of confidence.

> Change your posture to
> change your presence.

59

REFUEL YOUR FIRE

It was only ten A.M., but I felt like I'd already put in a full day. After an intense planning session with a business partner and a one-hour conference call with a hot prospect, my energy was sagging. Not good. I needed to finish a big project for a client. The deadline was looming, but I'd hit a stuck point and my mind was fried.

So I did what any self-respecting, stressed-out person does under pressure: I spent a few minutes reviewing my notes, then put on my tennis shoes and left the office. After a twenty-minute walk on a beautiful summer day, I returned refreshed. When I sat down at my desk again, I was clear on what needed to be done next. The bottleneck was gone. The project would be completed before the deadline.

While your time is a finite resource, your energy level is a renewable one. Slogging away at your desk isn't the answer to getting more done. Nor is pounding the phones all morning long without a break or working twelve-hour days.

You know what does help you get more done? According to

Professor K. Anders Ericsson of Florida State University, the best strategy for maximizing your productivity is to work in ninety-minute intervals. Beyond that, you run out of oomph, your mind wanders, and before you know it, you're futzing around online or grabbing a goody.

As a seller, your success depends on your thinking, ideas, skills, and insights. You need to be mentally agile, all day long. That's tough to do when our workaholic culture tells us that burning the midnight oil is what it takes to get ahead. But your body is physically incapable of delivering peak performance when you're pooped.

Refueling your fire is even more essential when learning so many new things. Here are three strategies you can use to keep yourself sharp and avoid burnout:

Get off your butt. Your body craves movement—and so does your mind. In fact, your brain actually works best when you're not actively thinking. Wander around your office. Walk the stairs. Go stretch somewhere. Get outside if you can, even if it's only for a short period of time. And take time to exercise at least three times per week for an hour. You will feel so much better and your brain will have an opportunity to rest and recalibrate as well.

Do something fun. This isn't a joke. Talk to your colleagues. Play some games. Give a friend a call. After fifteen minutes or so, return to the task at hand. When you're refreshed, you'll assimilate all that new information faster and will be able to rapidly improve your skills.

Get more sleep. If you're getting less than seven hours of sleep each night, your memory circuits are not operating at full strength. Your performance can be significantly improved by sleeping eight or more hours nightly. If you have a home office, you might even consider taking a midday nap.

Detach from devices. It's hard when they're your life-lines, but shutting down during breaks, evenings, and week-ends gives us a real breather. Turn off your cell phone for a period of time. At a minimum, don't check e-mail. Before you say it's impossible, give it a try. Even a couple hours of uncon-nected time is enough to renew your energy.

The chronic stress of overwork is debilitating and, it turns out, probably counterproductive. Several years ago, I read that French workers who put in thirty-six-hour weeks were more productive than Americans who averaged fifty-plus hours per week. Imagine that: Long hours and high stress levels do not equate to getting more done.

Take time each day to refuel your fire. When you do this, you increase your productivity. You'll be laser focused, better able to handle the ups and downs of your job.

> Manage your energy daily to
> perform at optimal levels.

60

PICK THE RIGHT ROLE MODEL

owell, Patty, and Beth. Without them in my life, I'm not sure what I'd be doing today. Maybe waitressing. Each of these individuals played a critical role in my sales success, although they were each totally unaware of it. They just did their jobs, but seeing them succeed mattered to me.

When I was hired by Xerox, I was excited, but scared. Survival was at the top of my mind. Many rookies never made it past the first year; sales was a brutal business with high turnover.

Fortunately, I met Lowell. He'd been hired just three months before me. When we talked, I discovered that he'd also been a teacher before moving into sales. He was doing okay in sales—not great, but he was meeting his quota. I remember saying to myself, "If Lowell can do it, so can I."

People always tell you to model yourself after the top people in your company, but I'm not sure that's necessarily the right approach. At Xerox, the experienced salespeople I met were a sharp bunch of go-getters, real pros. I could only hope that I'd achieve their level of success. Realistically, though, I wasn't sure if it was possible. The gap was too big.

But Lowell was real. He was making quota. Most important, he was close enough to my situation that I could see myself doing what he did. So I picked him as my role model. When I was struggling, I reminded myself that Lowell wasn't smarter or harder working than me—and therefore, if he could do it, so could I. Fortunately, over my five years there, Lowell kept getting better, and my performance improved along with his.

When I moved into high-tech sales, I was at a whole different point in my career. Although I'd mastered selling at Xerox, this new job was a big challenge. I had to learn a whole new language so I could talk to entirely different decision makers. The decision cycle was much more complex and significantly longer.

Before long, Patty became my role model. She'd started at CPT a few years before and was doing well. Like me, she was a technophobe. Her focus was strictly on selling the business case for change. Patty was great at getting both executives and end users to choose her solution over the competitors'. I knew I had those skills too.

When the tech talk overwhelmed me, I'd say to myself, "Hang in there, Jill. If Patty can do it, so can you." And I did, ultimately earning the International Rookie of the Year award. Without Patty, I would have been lost. She wasn't the top rep, but she was the right rep for me to model myself after.

Starting my own company took it to a very different level. As I was my own boss and sole employee at the time, I no longer had any colleagues I could use as role models. Fortunately, I moved into an executive office suite shared by a bunch of independent consultants. That's where I met Beth, an HR specialist. We had coffee together once a week and just talked.

Beth had been on her own for a couple years and was making it. She wasn't blowing it out with huge mega-contracts but she was earning a decent living. That's all I wanted to do. As peers, we shared ideas on a regular basis. What I learned from her helped and vice versa. But most important, I realized that if Beth could make it in this business, so could I.

Neither Lowell, Patty, nor Beth mentored me. We simply talked to each other as peers. They were ahead of me in their careers but not too far. They were doing well but weren't superstars performing at impossible levels. I could relate to some aspect of who they were. These factors all provided enough inspiration to keep me going when I was unsure if I could make it.

Take a look around at the people you know. Who could you pick as your role model?

> Choose role models who are slightly ahead of you in their careers.

61

RECALIBRATE OVER COFFEE

t's 8:03 A.M. I'm a few minutes late, but I know the person I'm meeting won't mind. I'm at this coffee shop, you see, for a serious conversation with myself. When the waitress comes, I order a cup of coffee and a cranberry scone, then get to work.

All I have with me are blank sheets of paper, a pencil, and an inquiring mind. Here's my challenge: One part of my business has slowed down recently. At first I assumed it would bounce back quickly, as it usually does, but this time it hasn't. I need to understand why it's happening, and what I can do to revitalize this revenue stream.

First, I brainstorm the numerous factors that could be contributing to the decline. I start a list, but don't like how it's going—it's too complex. I try a mind map instead; it allows me to doodle, which opens up more ideas.

I also discover that I need more data to figure out what external elements can be leading to this decline. Rather than stopping to research that now (and interrupting my thinking), I write down what's missing on a separate piece of paper.

Then I concentrate on the mind map, asking myself, "What could I do differently to get better results?" I doodle some more. I write down some obvious answers (increased activity, better targeting), but then go deeper into the challenge and approach it from other angles by changing the questions: "How can I get more of my best prospects to contact me?" "How can I leverage strategic relationships better?"

Now I have lots of ideas to play with, but I can't execute on them all. I need to figure out my best options. What can I implement right away to create a change? I also need a long-term approach to prevent it from happening again. I weigh the different options against each other.

Finally, I'm ready to put together a plan. I have a real clear idea on two things I'm going to change immediately. I'll actually start later this afternoon. In my plan, I've built in time for researching and talking to colleagues. I've also scheduled a meeting with Krista, my marketing director, for her input and help in implementing.

After two hours and multiple refills, I'm ready to head back to the office. Things were definitely off when I first sat down—now, I feel like I'm back on track. I've totally recalibrated over coffee and am leaving with fresh ideas that I know will make a difference.

I can't tell you how many times in my sales career I've done the process above. Sometimes I've been overwhelmed with everything I need to learn and do. Other times I've been in a slump or bent out of shape by office politics. I've even had serious conversations with myself about dealing with difficult customers and tough competitors.

As sellers, we're very action oriented. We don't stop to think about what we're doing; we just "do." Yet getting away from the office, the computer, and other people is often exactly what's needed to get perspective, to look beyond the obvious, and to come up with a rock-solid plan to address the challenges we face.

Tackling a new sales position isn't easy. To ensure that you stay on the right track, meet with yourself on a regular basis—alone, far from the madding crowd. When I do it, I always discover I know more than I think I do. Try it. You might be amazed at how much you really know too.

> Take time out to think and reflect,
> by yourself.

62

KEEP MOMENTUM GOING

Getting up to speed quickly can be both energizing and exhausting at the same time. What's crucial is that you keep moving forward, expanding your knowledge and fine-tuning your skills. To maintain both your impetus and your enthusiasm, use these strategies. They work!

Form a learning group. When you interact with other people, you learn a whole lot faster. At Xerox, there were a whole bunch of us who started at the same time. During our first year, we constantly tested one another. We brainstormed how to approach certain situations, role-played various scenarios, and reviewed one another's proposals. We even had a book club. Knowing that other people were in the same boat—and being able to bounce ideas off them—had a huge impact on my getting up to speed faster. If you work for a company where you have a peer group, form your own learning community. It'll really expedite your professional growth.

If you're on your own, you can use this strategy as well. I've created my own peer groups on numerous occasions. Several years ago, when I was just getting into professional speaking, I cofounded a group of five speakers who met monthly to practice and get feedback. The meetings were invaluable. Plus, it's something you can easily do on your own by inviting colleagues from within or outside your own company.

Revel in past successes. If your confidence is starting to waver, it's time to take immediate corrective action. Believe me, if you don't, it'll just keep eroding away. Start by looking backward, to times in your life when you've successfully overcome challenges.

Immerse yourself in those positive thoughts and wins for a while. Connect with your strengths again. When I was going through a major slump, my husband even said to me, "Are you ever going to work again?" I answered, "I think so." Getting my mojo back wasn't easy. I had to remember and revel in what I'd accomplished previously in order to give myself the confidence to address my current challenges.

Pat yourself on the back. All too often, companies reward salespeople only when they close deals. As far as I'm concerned, getting a sale is simply an outcome of doing many things right. What's most important, especially as you're learning, is to celebrate your achievements along the way.

Can you clearly articulate your value proposition now? What an achievement! Did you create a highly targeted prospecting list this morning? Yay, you're on your way! How about setting up three meetings today? Hip, hip, hooray! Did your conversation with your prospect advance to the logical next step? Good for you! Are you one of three finalists being considered? That's impressive. Movement matters. So does recognizing progress and being nice to yourself.

Read inspirational stories. When your enthusiasm is flagging and you're not sure if you're up to the challenge, look outside for support. Research into resilience is now showing that people who read about how others have overcome major difficulties in life will hang in there much longer. So when you're down, read about an athlete who made a major comeback, an entrepreneur who built an incredible business after three big flops, or a person who is changing the world despite a handicap. Knowing that others have succeeded against immense odds may be all you need to get your oomph back.

Being successful in sales is an ongoing challenge. Everyone wants to do well. When you're new to a job, it can be overwhelming. If you've been around for a while, dealing with all the changes can be hard. To keep on top of your game, you need to always be learning. Sometimes it's hard to stay motivated, but it is your responsibility.

> Motivate yourself to maintain your momentum.

Part 6

Final Words

63

CONCLUSION:
THE ULTIMATE CHALLENGE

There's never been a better time to be in sales. Despite the massive changes affecting our buyers, companies, and profession, we're on the cusp of an era when our success is defined by our willingness to invest in ourselves. The question is, are we willing to step up our game and become the differentiator?

By saying yes, you put your career on a new trajectory. You know that your knowledge and expertise matter more than your products, services, brand, or pricing. You know that your buyer's experience in working with you affects whether you get chosen—or not. You know that you're the one who's ultimately responsible for making that happen.

It boils down to this: To become the differentiator, you need to always be learning and growing. The faster you acquire new knowledge, the sooner you can leverage it. The quicker you can acquire new skills, the better your customer interactions become. You need to learn a lot and you need to learn it as expeditiously as possible.

Your learning agility becomes your competitive edge. You can ramp up quickly in any new position, becoming competent in record time. You can jump-start sales of new products or services into the marketplace. You can rapidly develop a deep and rich knowledge base. You can see multiple options to achieve your objectives and help your customers. To be an agile learner in today's business environment virtually guarantees a prosperous career.

Throughout this book, I've focused on strategies to help you assimilate both the knowledge and the skills you need to be highly effective in the shortest possible time. You might want to think about everything we've covered as part of Project You, an intensive program to fast-track your proficiency and achieve your financial goals.

The foundation for Project You is the agile mind-set. Remember, it all starts with a choice. Will you commit to sales success or not? If you don't make that commitment, there's a good chance you'll quit on yourself when the going gets tough—which it inevitably will.

By embracing the agile mind-set, you also learn strategies to deal with those difficult times. Instead of getting bogged down in problems, you create challenges you can solve. Instead of feeling like a failure when things don't work out, you embrace the many valuable learning experiences you're given. Instead of setting potentially demoralizing performance goals, you set "getting better" ones for yourself.

With this as your baseline for Project You, it's time to dig in, smartly. As we well know, your brain has its limitations. That's why if you want to get up to speed quickly, it's so essential to leverage rapid learning strategies. Osmosis is too slow. Training and onboarding programs are incomplete. And abdicating your sales development to someone other than yourself is foolhardy. If you want to make it, you need to own it.

In your Project You tool kit are the rapid learning strategies of chunking, sequencing, prioritizing, dumping, connecting, and deliberate practice. Learn these well and you're set for life. They're based on years of experience applying these techniques to the sales profession. You can use them in the first few months after you've been hired into a new sales position, if you're having trouble with sales and want to find out what works today, or when you're launching new products/services into the marketplace.

For Project You, I've also provided success habits for you to master. When you're on your path to proficiency, sometimes you need discipline and ideas that are outside your normal range of thinking.

Beware of complacency, however. You will reach a plateau where you're doing okay, and selling enough to make a decent living. Often, when you reach a level of proficiency, you stop learning and growing. Don't do that! It's going to kick you in the butt all too soon.

When you start to feel complacent, challenge yourself to get even better. Start by asking questions like:

- Am I having maximum impact in every interaction?
- What can I do to make it easier, simpler, or faster for both my prospect and me?
- What other options could I try to get the business?
- How can I reduce my losses to "no decision" or competitors?

Get curious again. Remember that sales is an experiment. It always will be. For long-term success, you need to stay in a testing mode. That's what leads to proficiency and, ultimately, mastery.

Are you up for the challenge? If so, know that it will be a rough ride for a while, as you pass through the valley of being overwhelmed. You're guaranteed to be out of your comfort zone, especially when you try to implement any new skills. You'll feel awkward and question your capability to adjust to the new world order. This is all normal. On the positive side, it gets easier over time. Soon you'll get really good at learning quickly and ramping up fast. This makes you even more valuable to your prospects and customers. Before long, they'll see you as an invaluable resource whom they need on their team. Ultimately, you get more business from them, fight fewer competitive battles, and become accepted as a peer.

Is it worth it? I sure think so, but the decision is yours.

> Make your own personal growth and development the number-one priority.

ACKNOWLEDGMENTS

It takes a village to write a book. And while my name is on the cover, it is only there because of the wonderful people in my life who've supported me on this journey.

First and foremost, my heartfelt gratitude goes to my husband, Fred, and our two children, Katie and Ryan. Their life is most impacted by my obsession with sharing my knowledge with the world. Without their support, I couldn't do it.

Many thanks to my clients too. I appreciate the opportunity to speak at your sales kickoff meetings and to train your sales teams. You keep me on my toes, constantly searching for ways to help you get more business with today's frazzled but very savvy customers.

For the 100,000-plus sellers who read my blog, subscribe to my newsletter, and watch my videos, I'm eternally grateful. You bring out the best in me. Every day I wake up thinking about how I can serve you better.

I am indebted to my marketing director, Krista Moon, and her team of Kevin Glatz and Tim Thyne. They kept everything running brilliantly while my attention was diverted elsewhere. Without them, this book might be coming out in 2020.

A big shout-out goes to the many awesome women in my life. Faith Ralston and Ardath Albee listen to my sometimes hare-brained ideas, inspire me to greater heights, and bless me with their friendship. Then there's my tribe, the Sales Shebang, an incredibly talented group of sales experts who keep cheering me on. A special thanks to Lori Richardson, Trish Bertuzzi, Colleen Stanley, Melinda Emerson, Kendra Lee, Barb Giamanco, Nancy Bleeke, Colleen Francis, Babette Ten Haken, and Nancy Nardin. You lift me up!

I also want to acknowledge these talented colleagues and friends who have stimulated my thinking, supported my work, and given me great feedback over the years: Dave Brock, Dave Stein, Jonathan Farrington, Charlie Green, Mark Hunter, Mike Schultz, Anthony Iannarino, Jonathan London, Michael Nick, Jim Keenan, Lee Salz, Sam Richter, Art Sobczak, Nick Miller, Miles Austin, Gary Hart, Bob Tersen, Craig Elias, Tim Hagen, Ken Thoreson, Kurt Shaver, Dan Waldschmidt, Steve Richard, and Jamie Shanks.

My agent, Ethan Friedman, deserves a big round of applause for helping me land a two-book deal with Portfolio, the best publisher in the industry. And kudos to my editor, Natalie Horbachevsky. She knows how to work magic with my writing.

Finally, I'd like to acknowledge myself. I know that sounds strange, but it's important. I did it. Becoming a leader in the sales field wasn't my goal. I just kept working hard, always striving to get better. I followed my interests, challenged myself to solve tough sales problems, and then shared what I learned with others. It's been a fun ride!

APPENDIX

LEARN MORE FROM JILL

FREE SALES RESOURCES

Below are the resources mentioned in this book. You'll find them, as well as many more, on the author's Web site at www.agileselling book.com:

- Buyer's Matrix
- Value Proposition Tool Kit
- Numerous Cheat Sheets
- *Hidden Gems* E-book

You'll also find more than seventy videos, a Prospecting Tool Kit, E-mail Sales Kit, and much more at www.jillkonrath.com/sales -resources.

CONNECT WITH JILL

Want to learn more from the author? Connect with her online via these channels:

- Web site: www.jillkonrath.com
- LinkedIn: www.linkedin.com/in/jillkonrath
- Twitter: www.twitter.com/jillkonrath
- Facebook: www.facebook.com/jillkonrath
- YouTube: www.youtube.com/jillkonrath
- Fresh Sales Strategies LinkedIn Group: bit.ly/Join-Fresh-Sales-Strategies

AGILITY-BOOSTING RESOURCES

Use these online sales tools and apps to research, connect, and build relationships with buyers.

SALES INTELLIGENCE

Build prospecting lists, find out how to connect, and discover invaluable information and insights about people and companies.

- LinkedIn.com
- Twitter.com
- InsideView.com
- DiscoverOrg.com
- Egrabber.com
- Data.com
- ZoomInfo.com
- OneSource.com
- Hoovers.com

- Rapportive.com
- GoogleAlerts.com

E-MAIL COMMUNICATIONS

Use real-time e-mail tracking and templates:

- GetSignals.com
- ToutApp.com
- YesWare.com

SALES MEETINGS

Set up virtual meetings and calls:

- GoToMeeting.com
- JoinMe.com
- Skype.com
- iMeet.com
- Glance.net

Create trackable presentations:

- Clearslide.com
- Brainshark.com
- PointAcross.com

PERSONAL PRODUCTIVITY

Organize and keep up-to-date:

- Evernote.com
- Pocket.com
- Feed.ly

Find a good time to meet:

- TimeTrade.com

Sign contracts quickly:

- Echosign.com
- Docusign.com

Avoid online distractions:

- GetColdTurkey.com
- Antisocial.cc
- SelfControlApp.com
- FocusBoosterApp.com

MANAGE YOUR PIPELINE

Cloud-based CRM (customer relationship management) systems to automate daily work and smartly manage your business relationships.

- Salesforce.com
- Nimble.com

- Insightly.com
- (Microsoft) Dynamics.crm.ms
- Zoho.com/crm
- SugarCRM.com
- HighriseHQ.com

BOOKS WORTH READING

SELLING

CONTEMPORARY SALES STRATEGIES THAT WORK WITH TODAY'S BUYERS. GOOD STUFF!

Act Like a Sales Pro, Julie Hanson, Career Press, 2011
Be Bold and Win the Sale, Jeff Shore, McGraw-Hill, 2014
The Challenger Sale, Matt Dixon and Brent Adamson, Portfolio, 2011
Conversations That Sell, Nancy Bleeke, AMACOM, 2013
Discover Questions Get You Connected, Deb Calvert, People First, 2013
Do You Mean Business?, Babette N. Ten Haken, Spinner Press, 2012
Emotional Intelligence for Sales Success, Colleen Stanley, AMACOM, 2012
High Profit Selling, Mark Hunter, AMACOM, 2012
Insight Selling: Surprising Research on What Sales Winners Do Differently, Mike Schultz and John E. Doerr, Wiley, 2014
The New Handshake, Barb Giamanco and Joan Curtis, Praeger, 2010

New Sales. Simplified, Mike Weinberg, AMACOM, 2012

Pick Up the Damn Phone, Joanne Black, Booktrope Editions, 2013

Pitch Anything, Oren Klaff, McGraw-Hill, 2011

Power Questions, Andrew Sobel and Jerold Panas, Wiley, 2012

Predictable Revenue, Aaron Ross, Pebblestorm, 2011

Rainmaking Conversations, Mike Schultz and John Doerr, Wiley, 2011

RFPs Suck, Tom Searcy, Channel V Books, 2009

The Sales Magnet, Kendra Lee, KLA Press, 2013

Selling to Big Companies, Jill Konrath, Kaplan, 2006

Selling with Noble Purpose, Lisa Earle McLeod, Wiley, 2012

Smart Calling, Art Sobczak, Wiley, 2013

Smart Selling on the Phone and Online, Josiane Feigon, AMACOM, 2009

SNAP Selling, Jill Konrath, Portfolio, 2010

Take the Cold Out of Cold Calling, Sam Richter, Beaver's Pond Press, 2009

To Sell Is Human, Daniel Pink, Riverhead Trade, 2013

White Board Selling, Corey Sommers and David Jenkins, Wiley, 2013

RAPID LEARNING | MASTERY

EXCELLENT RESOURCES FOR INCREASING YOUR SALES AGILITY; MY FAVORITE BOOKS

9 Things Successful People Do Differently, Heidi Grant Halvorson, Harvard Business Review, 2012

Adversity Quotient @ Work, Paul Stoltz, Morrow, 2000

The Art of Learning, Josh Waitkin, Free Press, 2008

Be Excellent at Anything, Tony Schwartz, Free Press, 2010

Brain Rules, John Medina, Pear Press, 2008

Brilliant: The New Science of Smart, Annie Murphy Paul, Crown, 2014

The First 20 Hours, Josh Kaufman, Portfolio, 2013

Focus: The Hidden Driver of Excellence, Daniel Goleman, Harper, 2013

Game Frame, Aaron Dignan, Free Press, 2011

How to Think Like Leonardo da Vinci, Michael J. Gelb, Dell, 1998

The Little Book of Talent, Daniel Coyle, Bantam, 2012

Mindset, Carol Dweck, Random House, 2006

Moonwalking with Einstein, Joshua Foer, Penguin, 2012

The Power of Habit, Charles Duhigg, Random House, 2013

Succeed: How We Can Reach Our Goals, Heidi Grant Halvorson, Plume, 2011

Thinking, Fast and Slow, Daniel Kahneman, Farrar, Straus and Giroux, 2011

The War of Art, Steven Pressfield, Warner Books, 2002

A Whole New Mind, Daniel Pink, Riverhead Trade, 2006

Your Brain at Work, David Rock, HarperCollins, 2009

INDEX